To Harvey,

From [illegible] rural north [illegible], thank you for giving me the opportunity to add that extra dimension to my life. I've had a wonderful ten & a half years in the department.

Warmly,

Eva

don't send me flowers
when I'm dead

To the people of this book and to my grandchildren.

don't send me flowers when I'm dead

voices of rural elderly

Eva J. Salber

Duke University Press   Durham, North Carolina   1983

Portions of this book are reprinted by permission of
The Gerontologist 20, 4 (1980): 421–26.

Printed in the United States of America on acid-free paper

Library of Congress Cataloging in Publication Data
Salber, Eva J.
 Don't send me flowers when I'm dead.

 Includes bibliographical references.
  1. Aged—North Carolina—Interviews. 2. Single
people—North Carolina—Interviews. 3. Farmers—North
Carolina—Interviews. 4. North Carolina—Rural
conditions. I. Title.
HQ1064.U6N525 1983   305.2′6′09756   82-21153
ISBN 0-8223-0529-1
ISBN 0-8223-0565-8 (pbk.)

contents

foreword · Robert Coles

This extraordinary book is yet another example of a growing tradition
—a literature of compelling and edifying oral history. Dr. Salber has
worked for years in one of North Carolina's rural areas, and doing so,
come to know certain elderly people rather well. She has attended their
physical complaints, but she has also wanted to know how they live,
what they hope for, and what they worry about. She has paid them the
tribute of attention—a serious, somewhat self-effacing regard. She has
asked them to speak on the record, so to speak, declare to others what
occurs to them in the waning hours of their particular lives. The result
is a series of American voices reminding us what it has been like for
relatively vulnerable, if not defenseless, southern country folk in this
rapidly disappearing twentieth century.

They are men and women, blacks and whites, Dr. Salber's teachers.
And they are precisely that—ready to educate a willing student, so
that she can carry such knowledge to the rest of us. Put differently, Dr.
Salber joins others, becomes a member of a particular tradition. One
thinks of Ronald Blythe and of Theodore Rosengarten and, of course,
Studs Terkel and Oscar Lewis—individuals who have, it can be argued,
tamed mightily the inevitable egoism we all must struggle with, so
that the omniscient observer and narrative writer gives way to the
eager listener and sensitive, knowing editor of messages offered, relatively unselfconsciously, by ordinary men and women who never once
thought their ideas, their apprehensions and hopes, would meet the
eyes of people called "readers."

I remember talking with a quite elderly Spanish-speaking woman in
the northern part of New Mexico. She expected to die a season or two
after our conversation was held. I told her I hoped to present her
statements to others, put them in a book, because I was so touched, so
impressed by what she had to tell my wife and me. She would have no
part, however, of my self-important promises, if not blandishments;
she was speaking out of the urgently felt imperatives of her life, and she

was perfectly content to let the worth of that life rest on its already accomplished deeds, rather than the suggested reward (if not glory) offered by an eager Anglo visitor. "What matters to me," she said rather defiantly, "is God's judgment." Then she went on to explain: "If He has heard me, over all these ninety years, then He has all the evidence, and I can only await His decision. And I am sure He *has* heard me! He hears everyone! Even now, I fear his decision. Will it be Heaven or Hell for me?" Nevertheless, for all her defiant rejection of all but divine evaluation, she was ready, upon occasion, for a glance at her fellow mortals: "I wouldn't mind telling a few stories to my children, and my grandchildren, and to my neighbors—stories they could remember, and tell to others. Is that what a book is—a way stories are kept from disappearing, when we disappear?"

Yes, Dr. Salber would no doubt have said, and then, waited and hoped: a few more of those tales from a wise and wizened (and sometimes wily!) old woman who, like the North Carolinians in this book, has no trouble giving us a good measure of open-eyed social comment, not to mention intelligent self-scrutiny and astute moral reflection. These pages glow with all that—the down-to-earth, yet often extremely suggestive and even provocative statements of those who have gone through this life at great length, and emerged, by and large, no fools about what goes on.

One concludes with a grateful avowal—a strong welcome to these voices, and to the doctor who has brought them to us. But one wants to go very much further—say that this book represents an intense and unyielding ethical as well as medical and literary commitment by a most impressive physician. Eva Salber has spent a lifetime working on behalf of this world's poor and persecuted people—men and women struggling long and hard against scant, even terribly cruel or punitive odds. In a better world, she would be one of America's heroes, as indeed would some of those whose words appear in this book—Americans who have modestly, insistently, laboriously tried to be good and decent and compassionate citizens. Godspeed, one wants to say, to all these elderly Americans, and to their most exemplary doctor, listener, friend.

preface

While all older people share certain characteristics and problems, circumstances of life for rural and urban elderly differ considerably. The urban elderly are an increasingly large segment of our cities' populations, and their problems have been given at least some media and political prominence. But we do not so often see the rural elderly who live in small, relatively remote communities, nor do we hear as much about the condition of their lives. The rigors of their lives in the absence of what we accept as necessary amenities and the fortitude with which this kind of deprivation is met may well astonish us.

The idea for this book took shape while I was completing a health study of two small communities in rural North Carolina. The book is about forty-five elderly men and women (thirty-three white and twelve black) who live alone in those communities and whom I have come to know over a period of six years. It is to the lives of rural elderly, as represented by this group, that my book is addressed. The book is based on a series of interviews with them which tell about their present lives, their remembrances of things past, their anticipations and fears for the future.

From the start, I had planned to present these interviews without adding my own professional comments, for it seemed to me that the participants expressed far better than I could their feelings, values, attitudes, desires, and needs. I believe strongly that their wishes and values must be respected and that we professionals must be wary of imposing on them our own values and standards in planning what we regard as solutions to their problems.

Along the way of the book's progress, interested friends have tried to persuade me that my comments and interpretations of events and data interspersed throughout the book would add a valuable "scholarly" dimension. But I believe that these comments should be as few as possible and that the facts, figures, and interpretations I have offered, providing a framework for the interviews, have an appropriate place only in a preface—the interviews speak clearly and eloquently for themselves. After all, a myriad of scientific books, government documents, and journal articles on geriatrics and gerontology are easily available.

In planning this book I was able to draw upon my past experience of close involvement with three communities. The first was in Durban, South Africa, the country of my birth, the second was in Boston, Massachusetts, the city to which my family and I immigrated in 1956, the third, Red Hill / Ashton, in rural North Carolina. My work with all of these people has had a profound effect on my attitude and my feelings as a doctor and a person.

As young clinicians, my husband and I enthusiastically undertook caring for the health of the people of an urban African township in South Africa, in a health center setting later used in the United States as a model for the Neighborhood Health Center movement. In this African township I realized that as important as medical care was to this malnourished community plagued with infectious and parasitic diseases, it alone was not sufficient for maintaining good health. Money, food, jobs, housing, and education were even more important.

In Boston, after nine years of research in epidemiology, I became the director of a family health center located in an inner-city housing project. As a consequence, my work and life became deeply involved with the lives of a low-income, predominantly black population. By this time experience had convinced me that active participation in the planning and organization of their own health services had a direct bearing on the physical and mental health of those being served and on the quality and nature of the medical care provided.

I used what for me was an untried technique to explore this concept more fully. Besides surveying, in the traditional "scientific" manner, the target population served by the health center, I interviewed some staff members and patients who lived or worked in the housing project, recording these unstructured conversations on tape. Eventually, I published a book reporting on their views, strengths, problems, and feelings.[1]

I have lived in North Carolina since August 1970 and have worked at Duke Medical Center for the last ten years. Here I have had no responsibility for providing direct medical care, as I did in Durban and Boston, but have been engaged in health-services research and community-

1. E. J. Salber, *Caring and Curing: Community Participation in Health Services* (New York: Neale Watson Academic Publications, Inc., 1975).

health education in the Department of Community and Family Medicine at Duke University.

Over a period of three years, my staff at Duke University and I conducted a household interview survey of the total low- and middle-income population of the adjoining rural communities, Red Hill and Ashton, collecting data on illnesses and the utilization of medical services. During the following three years, we analyzed and reported extensively on the demographic and socioeconomic characteristics of that population, the prevalence of illness, and the use of medical and dental services. During this period of data analysis, because I so often regretted that I had no record of the lives of some of our African patients similar to that of the people in my Boston study, I decided to record some reminiscences and personal impressions of life of the elderly in these two rural communities.

The two communities of Red Hill and Ashton occupy about sixty-four square miles in a county of the Piedmont section of North Carolina. Each locality includes a few country stores, a filling station or two, a small cafe, a post office, small, racially separated churches, small farms, tobacco barns, and single-family dwellings. The broad expanses of gently rolling countryside and clusters of massive hardwood trees provide a beautiful setting.

Driving down the wide highway, one is quite unaware of the many poor habitations hidden from view on narrow, unnamed dirt roads. There is no available public transportation for these residents, no bars, no movie theaters. On the whole, housing for whites is modest to comfortable. Housing for blacks is modest to quite inadequate; some old log cabins are still inhabited and many houses are in bad repair. There are a few large landowners, and new, substantial houses are beginning to spring up as town people move in. A sizeable proportion of families, particularly those that are black, lack the use of a family car, a telephone, indoor running water, or indoor toilet. In fact, more than half the black and about one-quarter of the total white population of age sixty-five or over live in households without indoor toilets.

About two-thirds of the total 2,250 residents are white and one-third are black. Many of the older individuals and their parents have spent their entire lives in the area. Education and income levels are somewhat below those of the county generally, with blacks poorer and less educated than whites. The white population is older than the black (at the time of the survey, 12 percent of whites and only 8 percent of blacks were over sixty-five years of age). A quarter of all residents give farming as their occupation, with tobacco the most important crop.

The population suffers from the same illnesses as those elsewhere in the United States, but residents, particularly blacks, use medical, dental, and preventive services less often than the national average.[2] No private doctor has an office in the area, but an outpost of the Neighborhood Health Center in the county seat has provided community care since 1972.

In the last few years the town has been encroaching on this rural area. It seems inevitable that it will soon become part of suburbia, and a particular way of life and traditions will be lost. Much is already lost except in the memories of the old.

It was to the old, and specifically to those who lived alone, that I addressed myself through unstructured interviews to questions about their lives and how they wished to spend their declining years. I asked all my interview participants to tell me about their early lives, their marriages, their work, what circumstances would make their lives easier and happier, at what period of their lives they had been happiest, their feelings about being old, and what they would do if they became disablingly ill. These questions were introduced during general conversation and not in any particular order.

Armed with a tape recorder, and with the aid of a loyal and dedicated assistant who knew the area intimately, I visited the forty-five persons identified as being low to middle income, over sixty-five years old, and living alone. Together we negotiated the potholes of narrow country roads and braved packs of dogs to reach the homes of our participants. I made my first interview visits in the fall of 1975 and returned about 18 months later for follow-up interviews. About a year after the second visit, I realized that photographs of the men and women I had interviewed—in their kitchens and living rooms, on their porches, working in the garden, attending church services—would add an invaluable dimension of intimacy and reality to the text. On yet a third visit, two talented friends who are photographers accompanied me. They took photographs while I revisited most of the group. During the fall of 1980 I paid a fourth visit to gather final material for the book.

During the course of these home visits I decided, also, to visit a few rest homes and a retirement home that boarded some of our area residents to explore reasons why some residents became institutionalized, while others remained independent. I did not visit nursing homes,

2. E. J. Salber, S. B. Greene, J. J. Feldman, and G. Hunter, "Access to Health Care in a Southern Rural Community," *Medical Care* 14 (1976): 971–86.

being reluctant to subject very frail, sick, and sometimes confused persons to my questions; I did, however, interview a nursing-home aide.

When the visits and interviews were completed, I was faced with the question of which interviews to include and how to edit them. I have chosen to present some interviews in more detail than others, because they seem to portray most clearly the character, quality, and individuality of the older men and women of Red Hill / Ashton and the circumstances of their lives. At least portions of every interview have been included.

I have changed the names of the two communities and of the people I interviewed as well as the names of their friends and neighbors. I suspect, however, that many will recognize themselves and smile as they did when they heard their voices played back on the tape recorder. Much of the interview material was gathered at the first interview, and the age recorded is the age at that first interview. Each person has given me permission to use his or her words and any photograph in whatever way would best serve the purpose of this book. While I have tried to reproduce, faithfully, the colloquialisms of the people, for ease of reading I have not attempted to give a precise phonetic rendition of their language (omitting, for example, the universal dropping of the g from -ing suffixes).

On our first visit, the people we interviewed couldn't believe that their lives would be of interest to us. Nonetheless, and without exception, they enjoyed the visits, felt they were too short, and invited us back. News traveled fast and many people anticipated our visits. Invariably, we were courteously received and were often the happy recipients of freshly picked corn, ripe tomatoes, home-baked cookies, delicious chess pies, and cuttings from plants.

Once started, they loved the chance to talk to people who regarded them as important and wanted to know about their lives. They showed us their photographs, wedding presents, plants, and handmade quilts. They asked nothing of us, but we often felt impelled to offer practical advice on how to get food stamps and Supplemental Security Insurance (SSI).

They talked of the past, of the days when they were not alone, and they talked with pride of how hard they had worked, for work had been, and often still was, the mainspring of their lives. Those who were still minding cattle, doing "day work," helping to bring in the tobacco crop, tending their yards, or putting up vegetables against the winter, felt useful. Some of them grew and put up far more produce than they could consume, for it was the habit of a lifetime, and proof to themselves that they could still manage. Sharing their bounty was their way of expressing neighborliness.

One of the participants told me that in the old days all you needed to farm the land was a mule and a strong back, but today, he said, you have to have a college education. In the mid 1930s, there were three-quarters of a million tenant farmers in North Carolina; in 1970, there were so few that "tenant farmer" could no longer be considered a significant census category.[3]

Whether or not they had continued to farm throughout their adult years, most of the participants in this collection had been children of men and women who worked the land. Some had been taken to the fields before they could walk; almost all had begun to work alongside their parents as soon as they could hold and wield a hoe. Tobacco was the chief cash crop; a vegetable patch, a few chickens, perhaps a hog or two, and a mule were necessities for sustenance. Most had been children of tenant farmers or sharecroppers, though a few had parents who owned the land. The son of a landowner usually inherited the farm and continued to work it; those who owned land were at considerable economic advantage over those who rented or sharecropped.

Regardless of status—owner, renter, or sharecropper—farming, and its unrelenting cycle of dependence on seasons and weather, determined the pattern of life. Farm work was a family undertaking, involving the help of neighbors and nearby kinfolk as well. As the land was tilled, the crops planted, watered, fertilized, weeded, and harvested according to the seasons, so the children attended school according to the needs of the crops. Many of the men and women interviewed were so constantly needed to help on the farm that they stopped going to school altogether after the second, third, or fourth grade. And as in their own childhood, their children, too, were often kept out of school. Work was always present and hard, but they were "used to it." The world of the farmer was encompassed by work, family, and church. Indeed, the life of the entire farm community revolved around a sharing of the same concerns.

Husband and wife were indispensable teammates. In many of the interviews, the men speak movingly and appreciatively of their wives'

3. A. F. Scott, Introduction to M. J. Hagood, *Mothers of the South* (New York: W. W. Norton and Co., 1977), p. vii.

hard work, help, and companionship. The women shared much of the heavy farm work with their husbands and took great pride in their own strength, endurance, and accomplishments. In addition, the women did all the "inside work," usually with the help of the older children — cooking, cleaning, washing, sewing, and taking care of the children — only "resting when it rained." And there were many children to take care of.

As hard as life was for the white woman, it was harder still for the black woman. In addition to working in the fields and taking care of her own family, she often supplemented the small family income with day work for a neighboring white family. However poor a white farmer, he could almost always manage to scrape up a few cents to hire a black woman to help his wife at corn-shucking or hog-killing time.

The New Deal, mechanization of farming, the advent of World War II and its promise of better paid jobs in war-related industries, were all responsible for the migration of huge numbers of men and women to the cities and away from precarious small-farm living. A large proportion of these migrants never returned to the land. Those who returned to North Carolina, typically, had low incomes and low educational levels.[4] For them and for those who remained, it has been an increasingly difficult struggle. Large, technologically operated, corporate farming has made the small family farm an anomaly. Between 1960 and 1964 an average of 376,000 people left southern farms each year.[5] Even so, at the time of my survey, 30 percent of white and 51 percent of black heads of household (25 percent of all residents) in Ashton / Red Hill gave farming as their occupation, (1.3 percent of the total county population gave farming as their occupation) for tobacco can still be, and was, cultivated by labor-intensive methods on small parcels of land. Often such farming was supplemented by part-time or odd jobs.

However, as the interviews reveal, almost all the children, and a few of the old-timers gave up the arduous life of farming for jobs in nearby factories (often tobacco), shops, construction work, hospitals, utility companies — jobs to which they generally refer as "public work." Few of these old-timers chose to move to town. Love of the land on which they and their parents had eked out a subsistence living, attending the church they had known since childhood, visiting with friends and

---

4. F. J. Ewing, "College-age and General Population Trends in North Carolina and the South," 1980. Paper presented at Annual Convention of North Carolina Association for Institutional Research.

5. A. F. Scott, Introduction to M. J. Hagood, *Mothers of the South*, p. viii.

neighbors whom they knew and trusted, and a suspicion of fast living and city ways kept them in their rural surroundings. Many of their children visit often and attend church regularly, but the grandchildren are drifting away from the old customs and values of the close-knit rural family and community.

An offshoot of an established urban organization, although a new type of organization for this community, gaining in popularity and located in the Fellowship Hall of a Methodist Church, is the Senior Citizens' Day Center. Lunch is provided at the center, women sew and are taught the usual handicrafts, men most often just sit and talk. It is a sign of the times that the day center is racially integrated, though participants still tend to sit and work in racially separate groups, for the social lives of whites and blacks are spent apart and their churches are still segregated. The religion of both races is overwhelmingly Protestant and predominantly Evangelical Baptist. Hill contrasts the southern white religion's focus on personal sin and salvation, and its deliberate disengagement from secular affairs, to the focus of European Protestant churches and their concern with social responsibility.[6]

The black church and its pastors have, however, always concerned themselves with secular as well as spiritual affairs. While much of black religion dwells on a happier life in Heaven, the church has maintained its historical role of being the one safe place in which to vent despair of injustice and to plan for a better life on earth. In spite of these differences, and despite the separate social lives they lead, blacks as well as whites have strong regional loyalties and identification with the South.

The elderly, both black and white, seem to accept almost unquestioningly the political, social, and economic dominance of whites in this society. (This is less true among the young of both races.) Black participants quite frequently mentioned white employers in recounting their life histories. Some black women talked fondly of white families for whom they had worked so long that they considered them almost as second families. White participants mentioned blacks who had worked for them, or for their parents, and at times they mentioned good black neighbors who willingly tilled the fields of old, frail farm neighbors at planting time. And one unusual participant talked of a visit to her

6. S. S. Hill, *Religion and the Solid South* (New York: Abingdon Press, 1972), pp. 24–56.

black friend in a nursing home. Indirectly, but without naming them, whites quite often referred to blacks when decrying welfare and scorning recipients of food stamps.

Whites referred to blacks almost without exception as "colored" men and women; almost never was the term "nigger" used in our presence. I sensed that keeping a discrete distance from whites is part of the usual behavior pattern of black men, less so for black women. In whites, I detected what might be considered a perpetuation, at least to some extent, of the "neo-paternalism" described by C. Vann Woodward as "a compound of philanthropy and unconscious condescension."[7]

Whether any half-conscious remnants of racial hostility play a part in their fear of violence, I do not know. But, certainly, fear of sleeping alone in their own homes and reports of occurrences of local violence were often talked about. Beneath the gentle manners and good nature of the people, a long tradition of southern violence and fear persists.[8]

A marked characteristic of these elderly people, particularly of the women, both during their working lives and during retirement, is their independence, their ability to manage alone. They had learned from childhood to be self-sufficient, to grow their own food, make their own soap, sew their own clothes, and draw sustenance from each other rather than from commercially manufactured goods and entertainment. Retirement to them does not have its commonly accepted meaning of "removal or withdrawal from service, office or business." In fact, retirement does not usually entail any drastic change in their mode of life, their pattern of living and working; rather, it means a lessening of the hours of work and an increase in the hours of leisure.

Retirement for women, their work load lightened, their money problems somewhat alleviated by Social Security, is often referred to as the happiest time of their lives. They continue to cook and clean, to see their children and grandchildren, to tend their gardens as long as they possibly can—even if it means sitting on a chair between the rows of beans—to put up produce, to sew and quilt, and to do the work that is familiar and meaningful to them.

Men have more problems with retirement. They are not used to "inside work" and have more difficulty taking care of themselves if left

7. C. Vann Woodward, *The Burden of Southern History* (Baton Rouge: Louisiana State University Press, 1968), p. 179.

8. J. S. Reed, *The Enduring South* (Lexington: D. C. Heath and Company, 1972), pp. 45–53.

to live alone. Vast quantities of eggs and canned beans seem to be staples of their diet. Few men adjust as well to a life without the usual pattern of working that has been set since childhood.

I was wrong at the beginning of my study in thinking that my target population of rural elderly, living alone in low-density areas, would suffer from the stresses of social isolation. Although many participants complained of loneliness, only one of them, a man, showed evidence of social isolation. As I learned more about the structure of Ashton / Red Hill, I began to realize that the pattern of community living protects the elderly from being socially isolated, and thereby strengthens their ability to cope with hardship. Much evidence has accumulated in the last decade which shows that effective informal social supports buffer, to a considerable extent, physical and mental aftermaths of severe stress.[9]

Informal support to the rural elderly is provided basically by their children and by other immediate and extended family members. This support is supplemented by concerned neighbors and long-time friends. Religious faith and regular attendance at church provides an additional source of support and helps to establish group cohesion and integration into the larger community.

Recent research data from several countries, including the United States, have discounted the myth that adult children no longer take responsibility for their parents.[10] Certainly among our participants, those who have children enjoy frequent visits from them. They turn to their children for help with shopping, household repairs, transportation to church, and assistance in visiting doctors and hospitals.

Though most are reluctant to move into their children's households, many of the men and women we interviewed live near a child or sibling. A few live in their own homes during the day but spend the night with a relative or friend. Several participants look out for each other: phoning or visiting every day, checking whether blinds have been pulled up in the morning, watching for signs of outdoor activity to be sure that all is well. Neighbors with cars regularly give rides to others who attend the same church.

9. B. H. Kaplan, J. C. Cassel, and S. Gore, "Social Support and Health Care," *Medical Care*, 15, 5 (1977): supplement 47–58; G. Caplan and M. Killilea, eds., *Support Systems and Mutual Help: Multidisciplinary Explorations* (New York: Grune and Stratton, 1976).

10. E. Shanas, "The Family as a Social Support System in Old Age," *Gerontologist* 19 (1979): 169–74.

To city dwellers who move frequently, the stability of small, southern rural communities like Ashton / Red Hill is surprising. Most of the older residents have lived in the same house since marriage or even earlier. Some have friends they have known since grade school with whom they continue to exchange visits, produce, baked goods, and community gossip. Many visit sick or housebound neighbors, prepare church dinners, attend quilting bees. Those who are able lend a hand in preparing tobacco for barning.

Both men and women seem determined to stay in their own homes. In one of my conversations with a very elderly woman I inquired why she and her twin brother didn't move in together. She told me that while each was willing to have the other move in with them, neither was willing to move into the other's house: "I have been living right here since 1917, this is home to me. When I leave here, you know where I want to go? To the cemetery."

Her brother spoke in the same way: "I love to be free. I've been free ever since I was married and got out to myself. The only one I had to listen at was my wife . . . . I ain't got nothing 'gainst none of 'em, but I just got to be in a house by myself."

The participants of this book have lived through a turbulent period of history. They or their parents have lived through two world wars, a devastating depression, the change from an agrarian to an industrial economic system, a gradual disappearance of legalized discrimination against blacks and an equally gradual acceptance of the principle of civil rights. They have witnessed the turmoil of the Vietnam War and have benefited from the Great Society Programs of the sixties.

Yet they seem curiously untouched by many of these events. Their conversations and interests are contained and localized. They talk of family and church, of crops and weather, of work, of food, of practical daily matters. Their intense ties to the land, their sense of place, are extremely localized. When asked where they live, they commonly do not answer Ashton or Red Hill, but refer, rather, to a particular small subarea of the already small township. Few have seen much beyond Ashton / Red Hill and the county seat. Over and over again, the outside observer is struck with the emphasis on and absorption in local life and affairs, the shared concern of a tightly knit social community—or perhaps two tightly knit social communities, white and black.

For some participants, despite strong community supports, increasing frailty had lessened the frequency of social contacts. Several who had thought little of walking many miles to visit friends or relatives became

XX

increasingly unable to initiate these contacts. Some could no longer attend church. Of those who suffered major illness, a few were fortunate in being able to remain at home, cared for by children, privately hired home helps, or by helpers provided by public agencies; others went to rest homes or nursing homes, usually after a period in the hospital.

While the elderly of Ashton / Red Hill who continue living in their own homes rarely experience social isolation, they cannot escape the emotional isolation which follows death of a spouse. For social isolation can be remedied or avoided by access to a social network; emotional isolation can be remedied only by the integration of another emotional attachment or the reintegration of the one that has been lost.[11]

Present-day rapidly rising divorce rates and frequent remarriages contrast sharply with the marital histories of almost all our participants. Of the forty-five, only two had separated and three had remarried. Most, married in their teens or early twenties, had worked together side by side, day in and day out until the death of a partner. This loss, sometimes after fifty years of close attachment, results in profound emotional deprivation. It must be understood that men and women of few other occupational groups are likely to have spent so much time together and with such close interdependence as dirt farmers.

Husbands express appreciation of their wives and talk of the magnitude of their loss even more movingly, vividly, and poignantly than do wives. Men seem to have more difficulty in adjusting to life alone, and the risk of dying after widowhood is greater in men.[12] Women do indeed express deep loneliness and sadness, but they show greater resilience and ability to manage on their own. They cling tenaciously to the familiarity and security of their homes, though children often offer refuge. Young grandchildren are a great source of consolation to all, and some find additional solace in deep attachments to dogs or other pets. (Regrettably, institutions usually do not allow their residents to keep their pets with them.)

The difference in ease of living among our participants who are poor and those few who are not poor is readily apparent in their conversation, their appearance, their housing, furnishing, and clothes. Though

11. R. S. Weiss, *Loneliness: the Experience of Emotional and Social Isolation* (Cambridge: MIT Press, 1973), pp. 227–36.
12. K. J. Helsing, M. Szklo, and G. W. Comstock, "Factors Associated with Mortality after Widowhood," *American Journal of Public Health* 71 (1981): 802–9.

the general pattern of daily living is not very different (certainly the contrasting styles of living among urban rich and poor is greatly diminished in this rural setting), a small increase in income seems to make a big difference in comfort and quality of life. For example, four of the twenty-six white women had owned cars and two still drive. Differences in lifestyle are most marked between whites and blacks.

A majority of white citizens appear to believe that most people on welfare have themselves to blame; they are on welfare rolls because of laziness or loose sexual morals. This attitude is shared to a considerable extent by many of our elderly participants, both white and black, who abhor welfare and often deny themselves food stamps because they believe this program to be a welfare handout. But some participants do not get food stamps for other reasons. They either do not know how to get them, or believe themselves incapable of completing the necessary procedures.

So they "manage," they make do, and they take great pride in their independence. Those who live in substandard housing, those who carry water from a distant spring, say it doesn't bother them, that they are used to doing this. Yet, when by some quirk of fate they acquire better housing or indoor plumbing, as happened to three of our participants, their pleasure brims over.

In some respects, though our participants are for the most part very poor, their lot improved during the years of our visits. The primary source of income for the vast majority of our participants is Social Security. Since the mid 1970s, with cost-of-living allowances being added to Social Security checks and the federalization of the Program of Aid to the Aged, Blind and Disabled in 1974, the lives of many elderly have become, not easy, but easier. Over the five or six years of our visits, and often through our intervention, several participants received SSI; their regular Social Security checks increased as inflation raised the cost of goods and services. Balanced against that, however, has been the unprecedented increase in the cost of home heating.

We do not have exact income figures for each household in Ashton / Red Hill. In our initial survey, we used a flash card displaying broad ranges of income (less than $2000, $2000 to less than $4000, etc.) and asked respondents to indicate the category which best fitted the total family income. Of our total sample of forty-five elderly persons living alone, seventeen of the twenty-six white women, four of the seven white men, *all* of the eight black women, and three of the four black men, reported incomes of less than $2000 in 1973.

North Carolina residents enjoy living in their state.[13] But it fares badly—forty-seventh in studies which measure the quality of life in the different states. Schwartz contends that in North Carolina the state's welfare programs fail to reach most of the poor. The vast majority of poor people are not poor because they are old, but poor because even though they work they do not earn enough to rise above the poverty level. North Carolina has the lowest wage structure in the nation and ranks last among the fifty states in average hourly wages paid to workers in manufacturing industries. In the last few decades North Carolina has changed from being a poor agricultural state to being a poor industrial state.[14]

National data reveal that a greater proportion of elderly than of the total population is poor.[15] In North Carolina, 25 percent of all elderly fell below the poverty level of $2791 set in 1975.[16] Certain categories of elderly are especially deprived: those who live alone or with non-relatives, women, and blacks. Thus the poorest of the poor are black, elderly women living alone; about two out of three are officially classified as poor.[17]

The situation is even worse in rural areas. Of the nation's poor elderly, 44 percent live in rural areas; 61 percent of them have 1977 incomes below $2000, and 81 percent below $4000; 5.5 percent have no Social Security benefits, and 3 percent have no income at all.[18] The elderly in rural poverty areas are not being adequately reached and serviced, and the asset limitations imposed by SSI eligibility criteria are not suitable for such populations.[19]

Cuts in social programs, especially Social Security, could have a devastating impact on poor, rural elderly. Despite the present tragic

13. Reed, *Enduring South.*

14. J. J. Schwartz, "North Carolina Welfare Policy: New Controversies and Unresolved Issues," in T. L. Beyle and M. G. Black, eds., *Politics and Policy in North Carolina* (New York: MSS Information Corporation, 1975), pp. 223–26.

15. C. S. Harris, *Fact Book on Aging: A Profile of America's Older Population* (Washington: The National Council on Aging, Inc., 1978), p. 43.

16. USDHHS Administration on Aging, *Facts About Older Americans* (Washington, D.C.: HHS Pub. No. [80-20006] 1980), [p. 2].

17. Harris, *Fact Book.*

18. P. K. H. Kim, "The Low Income Rural Elderly: Underserved Victims of Public Inequity." Paper prepared for the Community Service Administration Symposium on Policy Issues for the Elderly Poor, November 1980.

19. V. R. Kivett and R. M. Learner, "The Rural Elderly Poor: Economic Impacts and Policy Issues." Paper presented at the 33rd Annual Scientific Meeting of the Gerontological Society, San Diego, Calif., November 1980.

picture of elderly rural poverty, it is nevertheless true that elderly rural people reaching retirement age today are better off than their predecessors!

It would be wrong for me to convey a picture of deep gloom. I had not appreciated fully, before I met with them, that most participants enjoy living independently, express pleasure and pride in having lived so long, and want to go on living for many more years, despite their poverty.

I do not want to romanticize the lives of these rural people. Their lives are hard and have almost always been ones of unremitting toil with little economic return. Many of us might well consider their lives monotonous and narrow. But we must remember that their values, and their way of life, are different from the lives of those of us who study them and plan their care. Much could be done at small expense to make their lives easier: higher Social Security payments, insulation of homes, and installation of indoor plumbing, would increase their physical comfort and help maintain independent living. Provision of physical comfort in an institutional setting does not fit the pattern of their lives. The expectations of the elderly themselves, their values, their wants, their desires, must prevail. They are oriented to their own people and home place rather than to things. Their horizons may be narrow, limited in the main to kith and kin, neighbors, friends, and church, but their emotional attachments, their human relationships, their social supports in the community are strong and make their lives fulfilling.

But while life at home is fulfilling, one overriding and ever present fear is seldom mentioned, except after gentle prodding. People living independently fear the prospect of entry into a nursing home; if they must leave their own homes for an institution they prefer a "rest home." Most of all, they want home care, which is hard to come by and too expensive for most.

Indeed, the overriding reason for the recent intense emphasis on the subject of aging of our population is due to anxiety about the increasing cost of medical care services for the elderly. It has been said that in Great Britain health care is looked upon as a field of social cooperation, while in the United States it is considered a business.[20] Estimates of

20. C. Lockhart, "Values and Policy Conceptions of Health Policy Elites in the United States, the United Kingdom, and the Federal Republic of Germany," *Journal of Health Politics, Policy and Law* 6 (1981): 98–119.

future costs of health care for the total United States population are certainly staggeringly high,[21] and nursing home expenditures are absorbing an ever increasing proportion of Medicaid expenditures, despite the fact that individuals must first impoverish themselves before they become eligible for Medicaid.[22] But, as Robert Ball so aptly points out, it doesn't make too much sense for society to engage in providing doctors, hospitals, and nursing homes, unless people also have enough money for food and shelter.[23]

It is true that the typical nursing home is a much better place to be in today than it was a few years ago; it is, nevertheless, also true that nursing home residents tend to deteriorate quickly, both physically and psychologically. It is also true that residents are over-medicated and under-doctored. And roughly half the nursing homes are still substandard. While the effect on the lives of a small proportion of those living in truly horrible nursing homes is appalling, the aggregate harm done to a far larger resident population in thousands of homes that meet the minimal public standard is of far greater consequence and importance.[24] To quote Vladeck, "In these, residents live out the last of their days in an enclosed society without privacy, dignity, or pleasure, subsisting on minimally palatable diets, multiple sedatives, and large doses of television—eventually dying, one suspects, at least partially of boredom." He goes on to say that the existing nursing home industry is almost entirely a creation of public policy.

The image of a nursing home to most of our participants is the horrible kind, though some think more in terms of monotonous food and life, of curtailment of liberty and independence. Few regard these institutions as a solution to their increasing frailty. (Despite the presence of many chronic ailments, slightly less than half our participants rate themselves as in fair or poor health.)

It is of great significance for the elderly who live alone that a crucial factor in institutionalization is the absence of a spouse.[25] Typically, they enter a nursing home when the person who used to help them is

21. D. P. Rice, "Long Life to You," *American Demographics* 1 (1979): 9–15.

22. P. D. Fox, *Long Term Care: Background and Future Directions* (Washington: Health Care Financing Administration, 1981), p. 24.

23. R. M. Ball, "Rethinking National Policy on Health Care for the Elderly" in A. R. Sommers and D. R. Fabian, eds., *The Geriatric Imperative: An Introduction to Gerontology and Clinical Geriatrics* (New York: Appleton-Century-Crofts, 1981), p. 23.

24. B. C. Vladeck, *Unloving Care: The Nursing Home Tragedy* (New York: Basic Books, 1980), p. 4.

25. Fox, *Long Term Care*.

no longer available to do so. Entry into a nursing home is usually an act of last resort. And, indeed, most impaired elderly do not live in institutions; they live in the community, cared for by family and friends.[26] Interviews in rest homes with residents and their caretakers show clearly that the unmarried, the widowed, the childless are more likely to enter such institutions. The amount of informal support given by family and friends, coupled with the presence or absence of community in-home services, mainly determine whether or not the elderly leave their homes.

In conclusion, I have emphasized the themes of this book through interviews highlighting life in the old days, the marked independence of the people, the relationships between blacks and whites, the kind of work the people do, the poverty some of them endure, their community ties and supports, their loneliness when emotionally deprived, and their fear of being torn from their homes and loved ones in the event of a disabling illness.

The harsh change from a fulfilling, independent life at home in the familiar community to a life without purpose in the company of strangers, and in a different setting—what Blythe, in referring to refugees calls "being forced out of one's own landscape"[27]—comes through clearly in interviews with residents of rest homes and even from some of their caretakers. But sad as this period of change is, it points up even more clearly that the bulk of participants' lifespans have been spent in independence, with strength, self-discipline and endurance, with love, respect and pride, with kindness and humor.

In presenting these interviews I hope to achieve something that cannot be accomplished in scientific surveys. As valuable as health interview surveys are, they give only an aggregate picture of a community measured in statistical terms, and only the barest hint of the quality of individual human lives. It has been said that truth is more elusive than what a simple statistical count can establish and that statistics are people with the tears wiped off. Statistics alone cannot begin to convey the essence of human life.

The purpose of my book is to provide a channel through which this small group of elderly men and women transmit their feelings. I hope

26. Comptroller General of the United States, *Home Health—The Need for a National Policy to Better Provide for the Elderly* (Washington: General Accounting Office, 1977), p. 10.
27. R. Blythe, "Foreword," *Places: An Anthology of Britain* (Oxford: Oxford University Press, 1981), [p. vii].

their words will succeed in stirring the interest and concern of readers. Interest and concern, together with legislation and action, are essential if we are to provide the elderly with the comprehensive, community-based services needed to maintain them in comfort, dignity, and relative independence in their own homes as long as possible. If institutional life does become inevitable for some, concern and action are also needed to improve the quality of life in those institutions.

In the words of Eudora Welty, ". . . my wish, indeed my continuing passion, would be not to point the finger in judgment but to part a curtain, that invisible shadow that falls between people, the veil of indifference to each other's presence, each other's wonder, each other's human plight."[28]

28. E. Welty, *One Time, One Place* (New York: Random House, 1971), p. 8.

acknowledgments

Three foundations and many individuals have helped to make this book possible. The initial interviews were done while analyzing the data on a household interview survey of the area which was funded by the Robert Wood Johnson Foundation. The Lyndhurst Foundation and its executive director, Mr. Deaderick Montague, were particularly supportive and encouraging. They gave me the part-time salary and other support needed for completing the book. A much appreciated grant from the Z. Smith Reynolds Foundation enabled us to print the photographs which appear in the book. It would not have been possible for me to produce this book without the assistance of these three foundations to whom I am deeply grateful.

Dr. E. Harvey Estes, chairman of the Department of Community and Family Medicine, saw merit in my proposed task at its inception and strengthened my resolve to undertake the project. I thank him warmly for his continued interest in the work and the people.

Dr. Anne Firor Scott, chairman of the Department of History at Duke University, graciously agreed to preview the completed manuscript. I am grateful for her interest, warm support, and good advice.

I thank Professor William Bevan, provost of Duke University, who was kind enough to direct the attention of members of Duke faculty to my forthcoming book.

Among the friends who advised me, Dr. Jonathan Sher was particularly active and concerned.

Several secretaries labored over the six years transcribing tapes verbatim and typing repeated edited versions of those tapes. I single out for special praise three of them: Linda Grinstead, who began the work, Lynn Watson, who postponed accepting a more conveniently located job until she had finished typing the last word, and Pat Black, who produced the final draft on the word processor machine. I am exceedingly grateful to them all.

Inevitably, some members of my immediate family became involved and helpful in the work. My son, Mark Phillips, for many years has urged me to record my experiences with the different communities I have known and cherished. He also first urged me to seek out photographers who would add visual imagery to the unknown voices. My daughter-in-law, Juliet Phillips, gave valuable assistance in restructuring the final version of the preface.

Two men and three women have been of inestimable help to me over a prolonged period. Dr. Dominic D'Eustachio and Dr. Duncan Heron took the photographs that appear in this book. They graciously allowed me to use their free time, including Sundays, to go miles away from home and leisure in pursuit of the images I sought. Their work adds immeasurably to the value of the book, and I regret that it is possible to include only a small sample of their work.

Lucy Wilson, my good and long time friend in New York City, who struggled with me through the editing of my previous book, had the tenacity and courage to be my editorial assistant for the second time. When telephone and mail services proved inadequate for the task, she came to stay with me for two weeks, during which time neither of us got much sleep. Her personal commitment, intelligence, motivation, and integrity were invaluable.

I was indeed fortunate to have Betsy Zaumseil as a data technician during the analytic phase of the household interview survey. During that phase Betsy helped also in the preliminary editing of the interviews. After the funding of the survey ended, Betsy continued to help me in her free time. As a dear friend she found time to read through interminable versions of introductions and interviews, to help with problems of syntax and punctuation, and most of all to encourage me by her steadfast belief in the work and purpose of the book.

Most of all, I owe my deepest gratitude to Becky Heron, my warm friend and assistant who had been the chief interviewer in the original survey. She found the houses, made the appointments, chauffeured me, managed the tape recorder, and smoothed my path in every way. She was committed, loyal, and efficient; I could not have been better served.

I had the great good fortune to have Dr. Robert Coles agree to write the Foreword; it is a joy to have his words a part of this book.

Finally, there is no way I can adequately express what I have gained from the collective wisdom of the people whose interviews appear here. I can but hope that others may benefit as I have done from their friendliness, their kindness, their lack of greed, their patience, endurance, and stoicism, their steadfast values in a rapidly changing environment. It is their book as much as mine.

olden days

"In some ways the old days was better."

Ola Hill · 72 · "In some ways the old days was better."

Mrs. Hill is a tall black woman. When first I met her, her long, dark-complexioned face seemed plain, almost homely. She had many missing and carious teeth, which, four years later, were replaced with dentures (at a cost of $400). As I got to know her in the course of our interviews, I wondered how I had ever thought of her as plain; as she talked, her cheerful, ingenuous personality, and ready smile transformed her face.

The log cabin in which Mrs. Hill lives is reached by a very narrow, pot-holed dirt road. There are three rooms in the cabin, with a broad porch facing the road. Chinking between the logs is missing in many places; the inside of the cabin is lined with gypsum board in two of the three rooms, wood boards in the third. Mrs. Hill seldom uses her unheated living room which is neatly furnished with second-hand furniture. Her kitchen and bedroom each have a woodstove, one for cooking, the other for heating. The cabin has no electricity or gas, no running water or inside toilet, no telephone. Water for washing is collected from the rain in several large tubs at the side of the house. Drinking water comes from the well of a relative "at hollering distance" from her.

A childless widow, Mrs. Hill has relatives nearby and two dogs for company. Now aged seventy-seven, she is still doing domestic work.

My parents, they was raised here. They farmed, you know, 'bacco, corn, 'tatoes and stuff like that. Yes ma'am, on the white people's land. You know they had to do it. See, 'long then nobody such as me didn't own no land worth nothing 'cause we wasn't able. Our mothers had to wash and iron and clean up and cook and all such as that for the white people. When I's little we'd just play around with the white children; we grew up together. This boy that runs this post office up there, well now I toted him around when he was a little baby. When I was big enough to help a little, we had to pull suckers out of 'bacco, pull fodder off the corn, and pull corn. Back there in them olden times there wasn't very much; you had to do everything just with your hands.

I didn't get to go to school very much, I just went enough to learn how to read and write a little. You see, my parents was poor, and you know they wouldn't punish you for keeping children out of school then. Poor folks had to keep they children out to help do what little they had to do at home. 'Long then they boiled clothes in those big old pots and you have to drag up brush and stuff to keep them clothes a-boiling and all. The young say today, "Well I couldn't a done that." I say, "Yes you would have done or got whooped one!" I wish I had the opportunity to go to school like children do now.

I worked around a little till I got married when I was good and grown in 1934. My husband been dead 'bout—let me get the Bible if you don't mind—I have worried so much 'bout my mama and all, looks like sometimes I ain't got a good mind. My mama will be dead twelve months this coming Wednesday 'fore the first Sunday in December. My mama was 'bout a hundred years old. She was old so she came over here to stay with me. She could manage to sweep a little and do light dishes and things like that till she got down; she had a stroke. I nursed her 'bout six or seven months; she didn't want to go to a nursing home. I tell you, she's got a cousin been in a nursing home, and mama had been down there to see her so much; that kind of disgusted her. I kept mama here; she wanted to stay at home. I taken her down to Mill Town Hospital two or three times but they said they couldn't do her no good, said she had a cyst that would have to call for an operation. So he told me to give her some medicine and for her to take her time. She didn't suffer so much, she just had little bad spells at times. I didn't mind waiting on her. Finally, for 'bout three or four weeks, she just got helpless like a baby. Her sister would come down here at night and stay with me and help. I would get up all through the night. I didn't mind doing it at all.

I been working for the B——'s a right good while, ever since they come here. When they first come here the train was running—Mr. B was a depot aide. She was so nice to me when mama was down sick. The family is just as good to me as they can be. When my legs was hurt, fractured my ankle, Mrs. B carried me to the doctor all the time. They do anything they can for me, just as nice as they can be. She invited me to eat dinner with her last Christmas. The baby boy is grown now; he was twenty-one this year. I iron a little few clothes, clean up the house. I don't work every day. I stay home near 'bout one day out of a week and sometimes two days out of a week. Some days I work just part of a day and get my own little work caught up when I come on home. That keeps your mind better, you got something to do. I got to go out and do a little something, and that keeps your worries off. 'Course things will run across your mind, but still that keeps it off somewhat.

When you came the first time I got $94.20 Social Security. Now I get $140 some. No, I don't get food stamps—I just didn't have no way getting up and down the road. But me and mama managed to eat a plenty when she was living and Mrs. B always fixes me something out of her garden and gives me. When I get my little check I have to go to the store. And I finally got that gold check (SSI) you told me I could get. But I have a little 'bacco crop, my niece works it, and the little money I get out of the crop these months they cut off the gold check and then they'll start it again. I come to Mill Town to report what I get from my little 'bacco crop, and I cain't go over the amount when I'm working for Mrs. B. They have a limit and if you work over it, you got to pay that back. I went over one time; we wasn't keeping up with it. We try not to go over, and some weeks I don't have to work everyday. I get $15 a week.

I do pretty good. You see I have money to buy my little food, buy my wood. I tell you how come I buy my wood. I got wood on my place, but time I pay somebody to cut it and pay somebody to get it to the wood pile and pay somebody to haul it and all, it just costs me more. So I just buy my wood already cut. When you ain't got nobody but yourself when you have things to do, it ain't as easy as you think it is.

I ain't never had no light put in here. After my husband died, you know how you feel. 'Course you ain't never lost nobody that close, you married? The house ain't never been finished. . . . I use to get water in hollering distance from me, but the well's 'bout to go dry now. Now I totes water from up here at the trailer house; it don't take long to walk, 'bout ten minutes, if I ain't in no hurry. I totes three buckets of water, then I get four jugs.

I don't hardly ever get lonely. Well, I tell you, when my husband died I had somebody in the house with me, and the young folks was just in and out all the time. See, I never had to be bothered with people in and out before, I just rather be by myself. I always mess around here and do something all the time. I go out and sit and talk to my dogs. I like 'em, they company to me, I talk some to 'em when I'm down, they glad to see me. I bring me in some wood. I always plants me a hill or two of tomatoes around here somewhere in the yard. Just first one little thing to another.

I goes to church on Sunday. Everybody around here from children on up is members. Church means a whole lot to you if you go and take it in the right way. It makes you think about the Lord, how to serve the Lord, or how to treat people, and the way you would wish for people to treat you. God have brought us poor folks from a long way. Course you don't know nothing 'bout that, 'cause you ain't poor, but He have brought us from a long way. He's made it where young folks can get out and live good if they any 'count. I hate to say it, but God is brought things good to us poor folks and I'm mighty scared in just a few years He going to cut it off, 'cause it looks like the young folks ain't 'preciating it. I don't know what's the matter with 'em, some of 'em. The young folks they go down to church, but I say sometimes they oughta be at home 'cause they ain't putting it to no good use. They'll go to church, but time they hit that house they got some old song on that record player. It ain't no Christian song. They done been to church and time they hit the house they got that thing on. And I'll say to some of 'em, "Well, why don't you put something good on the record player? It don't pay you to go to church, if you don't think about the Lord no more than that."

In some ways the old days was better. Now, our parents didn't have much money but do you know they 'preciated what they did have. You don't know it, 'cause you didn't come 'long way back yonder, but they sure Lord did. What I mean by that, look like everybody was loving. Now you take some of my color, the young ones, they'll walk all over you, won't even say how you do. Been knowing you all they life and they just walk all over you if you didn't get out the way. I don't know what's the matter with 'em. They just ain't got what they oughta have. I don't think they care too much 'bout old people, do you? Some of 'em sassy to their mamas and daddies. I ain't use to that. And some of the young folks look like they got a job, they don't want to stay on it, it's too hard working. You got to work to live. You got to have some money.

My married life when my husband was living was the best time. After he died I just—you know how you feel. After he died we had debts. We had a little insurance, but he had to go to the hospital; he stayed one month and three weeks. I just had to go to work and try to pay them debts off. The hospital was four thousand and something. I think they give me one thousand off outside those doctor bills and all. I just paid by the month 'bout forty dollars. Last month they said they wasn't due no more and they sent the check back. I 'preciate them giving me time to pay it.

Life now? Well it is pretty good at times and sad at times. I wish my husband and mama was back here. That would be my wish, if it was possible.

If I get sick where would I go? Well that's a question, ain't it? I think 'bout that myself, I do really think 'bout that myself. I tell you what I says to myself. That's my folks over there, that's my sister's [Georgia Brown] boy and this last trailer you passed, that's my sister's son. Then right over 'cross the branch over there, that's my sister's son also. But when you mama's dead and your husband's gone, you feel like you ain't got nobody sometimes. I feel so bad sometimes. It would be nice if you had somebody, but you don't never know who going stick when times come like that; it's a problem. If I just get real down sick I feel like I would have to go to the rest homes. They're nice places, don't you think? So in a way when you get so you really cain't do for yourself, probably nobody you really can depend on, don't you think that's a good place? But I hope I won't have to go to a nursing home. I have the little old home and I thought probably if I didn't get too sick, I would probably give it to somebody to come live with me. Ain't that a pretty good idea?

Sally Woods · 79 · "Right now they're tramping on your toes, but when they get bigger they'll be tramping on your heart."

Mrs. Woods, a gray haired, fair-skinned woman, walks with difficulty but seldom uses her walker because she "doesn't want to get used to it." Her back is crooked from arthritis, most of her joints are affected. Despite her arthritic hands she still sews, and lovingly tends her forty African violets and numerous other potted plants. A son now owns and cares for the white, two-story farmhouse in which she lives. An attractive railed porch stretches across almost the entire front of the house. Across the road is a pond which allows Mrs. Woods to indulge in her favorite pastime of fishing.

Even with some help from her devoted family, Mrs. Woods is barely able to manage financially, but she cherishes her independence. A little embarrassed to admit to dipping snuff, her ceramic spitoon was almost concealed under her favorite chair.

I been living in this county more than sixty years. My daddy was raised in Parson County, not too far from here. He run a gristmill.

There was eighteen of us children, nine girls and nine boys. I was next to the oldest girl, but she died when she was two, and I helped tend to the children and do what I could at my age. I didn't get to go to school much; I reckon I got to the first grade. When I was eight years old I was big enough to wash diapers, and on up to ten I started to wash the regular washing.

It take 'bout a day to wash the best clothes, and the colored clothes we'd wash them the next day. It'd take all day, the next day to iron. We got water from the spring way up the hill, 'bout half a mile. We carried buckets and the small 'uns who could tote a gallon bucket, we'd make 'em tote too.

We cooked with that water, bathed children, done our own bathing in it. We heat the water in a great big old iron pot. But when we washed clothes in it we poured the water out, didn't use it no more.

We made our soap from dried meat skins and things like that and with lye. We boiled the sheets the children sleep on and men's underwear and diapers. And men's overalls, they was so dirty, good golly, had to scrub 'em on a washboard.

My father didn't have a farm, but we had a big garden and raised two cows and a horse. I helped pick and shell beans and tote in wood for the fireplace. We cooked in the fireplace, hung the pot on a hook, had a big black kettle for water and a skillet to cook bread in.

When I was eighteen I got married. I thought my life would be easier, but it wasn't. I married a farmer and had eight children and had to work in the field and I never worked in the field on the farm before. I done everything except plowing. I wouldn't do that 'cause I thought I was doing enough without plowing. We'd have to get up at two o'clock in the morning and empty out a barn of tobacco, come back to the house and eat breakfast and then be back in the fields by sun-up. And then bathe the children and get them to bed, and get supper on the table. Get to bed about nine or nine-thirty.

I'd cook enough vegetables for dinner and supper and put the supper vegetables in the oven to keep warm. I'd cook 'bout fifty biscuits for breakfast and again fifty for supper. We had cows and plenty of butter and milk. Supper was mostly buttered biscuits and snaps [string beans] and corn, or anything like that left over from dinner. We killed hogs every fall and we had fried ham with the biscuits. After supper we string the little tobacco sacks 'fore we went to bed. When the children was big enough to turn the sacks they helped me. We'd get 30 cents for a hundred. They would come in a great big bag, be 'bout a thousand little sacks in a bag and they was all sewed together. We'd clip 'em, turn 'em and string 'em. We thought we was getting rich when we string a whole big bag full. You could buy something for a dollar then.

We didn't buy no groceries; coffee and sugar was 'bout the only thing we did buy. I traded eggs and chickens for that and if I wanted to spend for something for my own. My husband was suppose to help clothe them children. We went to the country store anytime we needed anything. They sold cloth and most anything you needed. I had a sewing machine. I sewed for myself, my husband's shirts and underwear, and clothes for all the children.

We went on the train to Mill Town 'bout onc't a year before Christmas to buy toys for the children. Every Sunday we'd take the children to Sunday school and church. We rested when it rained!

Yes, I spanked the children. I started spanking the children when they was teething. While I was nursing them, they would look up at me like that, close their mouth and look up, they was fixing to bite me and I'd spank them before they'd bite! When they was big enough, twelve or fifteen months, I'd take them to bed with me 'cause I didn't want them to get out. I'd have two or three small ones in the bed with me and they'd get to laughing and cutting up. I'd smack one and turn over and smack another one real hard and make them cry and I'd say, "You better be still"; it wouldn't be five minutes they'd be asleep.

I went on spanking till they was big children, twelve or thirteen. I whooped them up till that. That's the only way you could make them mind then, but you don't do that now. It was something to raise children back then, but it's a whole lot better than raising them now. 'Cause now they tell old people what to do.

My daddy always told me, when they'd get to crying and I'd have so much to do and they'd want me to stop and hold them, "Right now they're tramping on your toes, but when they get bigger they'll be tramping on your heart."

The most important thing is to stay by myself as long as I want to. I enjoy fishing, and I like to sew, and I like to fool with flowers. I been so busy canning, my flowers needs watering right now. Keeping house is my biggest problem. Just keeping my yard mowed and toting out the garbage—that's a job too. It certainly would help to have somebody come in to help. I was watching a program on T.V. the other night where they had someone come in and mow the yard. I don't think I'd be able to pay for it, though, 'cause everything's gone up so much.

What do I want for myself, right now? I just want to be able to wait on myself. I don't want to put myself on my children. I don't want to be a bother to nobody.

Lola Buchanan · 70 · "People are not so happy now. You cain't even stay home to raise your children."

Mrs. Buchanan lives in a dilapidated, unpainted frame shack. The rail of the stairs leading to the front door is loose, the stairs themselves are rickety and unstable. The screen door hinges are bent and loose. Once inside the house, the living room, bedroom and kitchen are neatly furnished and cheerful. Numerous framed photographs of her family are displayed on walls and tables, and samples of her crochet work and sewing brighten her small living room. An empty coffee can stands at the side of the chair she usually sits in; Mrs. Buchanan regularly dips snuff.

A light-complexioned black woman, Mrs. Buchanan is small-boned, thin and wiry. Each visit found her engaged in some activity: handwork, canning or gardening.

I don't exactly know how old I am; I reckon I'm about seventy now. When I was small life was pretty hard, but it seemed good to us when we was coming up. Well, you know, in a big family you generally have a plenty to eat, but you never go anywhere hardly ever, just sometimes. That was way back yonder in the olden days. Yeah, it was hard living but we had plenty to eat. My father killed hogs, he'd kill a cow, have sweet potatoes in hills, have white potatoes, turned down collards. We'd pick peas in the fall of the year and butter beans.

You'd get up about four o'clock and get breakfast and when it get light enough, get out there and get to picking cotton. Get that dew crop—it'd weigh heavy. When I was grown, I have picked as high as four-hundred pounds of cotton in one day. Your back get tired bending and then you crawl on your knees; you have knee pads on. You grab a mouthful to eat and keep on picking. You start picking in September and then you pick till it be cold weather, and you still be picking your cotton. You stop about six o'clock, cook your supper and then put your dinner on for the next day. The rest of the year you sit around and quilt quilts until you get so cold you couldn't do nothing.

I reckon I got to the second grade in school. Of course all my children I sent them to school and they finished. If I have to sign something I get my children to sign it.

I was sixteen when I got married and my husband worked at the sawmill. I worked around wherever I could get work at. I did day work. Sometimes I worked for somebody or ironed, maybe picked cotton; got paid by the hundred, a dollar a hundred pound. I have chopped cotton a many a day for fifty cents when I was young. Day work pay a dollar fifty.

The best time of my life is now. I ain't got nothing to worry about. No children to get out and no boys running and ripping and me wondering what is he into. I have plenty to eat and I enjoy staying here by myself. Best time of my life.

I just do first one thing and then another. I work a little bit, day work, every now and then, not every day. Some weeks I work two days and some I don't work but one. But I get out here and walk six or seven miles anytime. I go up here to my daughter. Time I walk up there and back it's a lot of miles. I reckon that exercise helps me. I walk to Ashton anytime and back, sometimes twic't a day. I runs the power mower. It don't bother me. I can do just as much work now as I ever done in my life. If I want to get through in the garden, I go in there and work all day in it. I go to church every preaching Sunday.

In the wintertime, I just fire the heaters and sit back and sew. I crochet. I made me a bedspread and several little things, pillows. Turn on the T.V. or radio, that's all the fun I want. There's nothing I want; I'm just as comfortable as I want to be.

I don't have any running water inside the house, I have a spring right out there across the road. My grandson he comes every week and tote me up some water. 'Course I goes down there and get water myself when I needs it. I have an outhouse, but some mornings if it's real bad I just go stay with my daughter till the weather breaks. It would be nice to have some things, but I've always been use to this and it don't go hard with me. I don't miss what I don't have. I reckon I am old-timey.

The old time is better than the new time. To an old person like me what done growed up, the old way seems better than the new way. The new way is fast times. People are not so happy now 'cause they work themselves to death. Ain't that right? You cain't even stay home to raise your children; you got to be out at work and other folks raise them. That's right. I stayed home with my children, stayed right there with them. I never let my child go out and stay a night in their life away from me. I picked cotton and had my baby sitting in a box, and I'd push the baby up the row and pick up to it again and push it back up the row. I've done that many a time. Wherever I was, day work, my children was. Yeah, there's a lot more work going on now than there was when I come up. I think folks catches it tougher now than they did then.

I don't need to go to a doctor. It's time enough for me to go when I get sick. I don't think I've saw a doctor but twic't since my husband died, and he been dead way over thirty years. I had the sore throat then, tonsillitis sore throat, and I went to him, and then my back got to hurting and I went to him, and that's all.

When I get so I cain't look after myself, my children will look after me. I want to be next to my children. I don't want to go to a nursing home. Some of them folk would tear your rump up. If I didn't have children, I would hire some good person to come in. I worked over there fifteen years straight for Mr. Cooper. He was sick and his wife was sick. I went there and I kept house, cooked, cleaned up, and seed after them for fifteen years. Sometimes he'd run away and I'd have to go out and look for him. One night he was sitting right flat in the branch [creek] and couldn't get up. I called the children and they come and looked for him till they found him. The old lady was just as sweet and nice as she could be, but she didn't know her own children. I'd cry sometimes. I'd say, "Lord, I just cain't stay here, nobody to talk to," and you know she looked like she was going to die every minute. But I stayed there till she died. Mrs. Pearl's mommy—I waited on her. I waited on Mrs. Lewis. I have waited on a lot of folks. When I was a young girl, I would wait on people. Folks ask me to help now, but I done do that enough. All the white folks just as good to me as they can be. Everybody round me, they call me, but I don't want no regular job now.

I got plenty grandchildren, about forty; I don't know how many great [grandchildren]. All of them comes together to see me on Christmas. Feel old? No, I don't feel old. Some younger than I is done gone on. But the Lord's left me here a long time. I think it's nice to stay here that long.

Bessie Watson · 84 · "Then there would be mobs and mobs at church. Now, they will stand in line to go to a show."

Mrs. Watson's appearance is not consistent with the way she describes herself, "I'm crooked as a rainbow . . . it'd take putty to fill my wrinkles." The wrinkles in her face are not pronounced, she carries her slim, tall frame erectly and moves with vigor. On each of our four visits, the last when she had just turned eighty-nine and had recently had a cataract operation, Mrs. Watson was carefully and attractively dressed. Her daughter, whom we met on two of our visits, comes to see her mother at least once a month. At our last visit the daughter commented approvingly that her mother hadn't lost her pride. At each visit, Mrs. Watson reiterated her determination to remain living alone in her own home.

Mrs. Watson's freshly painted, white, two-story frame house faces a well-traveled paved road. Across the front of the six-room house is a wide porch bordered with shrubs. Her colorful flower garden at the back of the house, with its array of bulbs, is particularly attractive in the spring. The living room in which we sat was comfortably furnished with solid furniture inherited from her parents and grand-parents.

I got married when I was nineteen and went to live in Virginia. My husband was an agent for the North Western Railroad. I had two children; the oldest, the boy, is dead now. My husband died with a heart attack about five years after we were married, and I came back here to stay with my father. He looked after me and helped me with the children. My father farmed and then he worked in the store and he was a carpenter, a jack of all trades. I've been in this house about sixty years and been living alone six years last month. My son lived with me until he passed away. My daughter lives about one hundred-sixty miles away, but she comes here every three weeks or so and whenever I need her.

I kinda had to do for myself after my son died. I didn't know what a bill was or nothing, not even my insurance until he died. I never worked nothing before but housework and gardening. Shucks, hard work haven't killed me. If you are able to work, it helps you keep going. I ain't complaining; I've had right good health. You sit down at my age, you will sit there; I ain't sitting in a rocking chair yet. I work in the yard when it's not too hot and I had some right pretty roses, but old people and flowers don't go together. I just let them go now. This colored man he come here, he's the main help. I have a woman who cleans good about onc't a month. I don't keep house, the house keeps me now, but I sweep up and do things like that though, and I got a little boy who comes and mows my yard. Of course I do all my own cooking and I still bake my biscuits. I don't want to live with anybody, because I'd rather be home. I don't think any house is big enough for two families, I don't care who it is. And I have neighbors that's just as good to me as my daughter is.

I reckon the happiest time of my life was when my children was small babies coming on up. I enjoyed them. I enjoyed my own child-hood too. We didn't expect so much like the children do now; today they wouldn't even stay home for what I had. Oh, I just went to church, Sunday school—that was an attraction to children then, going to Sunday school. Now they wouldn't be entertained like that. You know then there would be mobs and mobs at church. Now you don't see that. They will stand in line to go to a show, but you don't see anybody standing in line to go to a church. Children get too much now. I just had the average goodies as any of my neighbors had. Back then, well, you don't know nothing about then, that was horse and buggy days. Going to Mill Town was more than a child now would think about going to New York. Took all day. Went in the morning, usually come back the next day. Out of one mud hole into another. I know you've been out on a country road. Well, the country road now is better than the old road was from here to Mill Town, and if people with tobacco went today they would get back tomorrow night.

The young folks had parties, pulling candy, dancing, and things like that. I had a time or two. I don't know about my real parents. I was adopted and the only child. But if you knew my mother! I was never allowed to go to dances. My mother was against dancing and card playing, she wouldn't have a deck of cards in her house. If she found a deck she would put them in the fire. She was just that way and most old people was like that then. I went to picnics and there would always be a chaperone to look after you. I don't care where you went, there would be a chaperone to look after you.

After I was through with high school, my mother was sick and I had to see after her and do for her. Back then they didn't have places to put people. When anybody got sick you waited on them at your home until they passed away. Now when they get a little illness, least nothing the matter with them, they put them in a home somewhere. I told my doctor, "Don't you do one thing to prolong my life." He said, "Miss Watson, I'm going to do what I want to do." He's been my doctor for eighteen years. I was over to see him one Christmas and he said to me, "Too cold in the cemetery now, Miss Watson!"

Elizabeth Lee · 72 · "I nursed all my children till they was three years old. Nowadays mothers wants to work all the time."

Mrs. Lee's house is at the end of a lonely dirt road about one-half mile long. Her son is building a house across the road from her, but at the moment she is quite isolated. She is used to living alone although she very much misses not having someone to talk to and to take her visiting and shopping. The house, well kept, clean and neat has four small rooms. Cooking is done on a gas stove; an oil circulator heats the house; there is no bathroom.

Mrs. Lee, a thin, black woman is reserved and unassertive. Her shy smile reveals several missing teeth.

I was raised on the farm; know nothing else but farming. There was ten of us children in all. We started very young with such as picking peas and helping Mama in the garden and all like that. After I got big enough, I picked tobacco. We had to get up early and get out in the field around about seven o'clock in the summertime. We stopped for lunch, about an hour for rest period and we'd go back in the field till sundown. Then we'd have supper and I helped in the house. Mostly my job would be washing dishes. We'd sit around and then go to bed.

It hasn't been no easy life. My mama and daddy was tight on us—now the young people won't stand for that. We didn't have a chance to play much through the week. On Sunday we'd have our little fun running around, playing ball, and going through the woods looking at the river or something like that. In the winter after we got big enough we'd go to school. When we stayed on the other side of the river we had about a mile to get to school. Then after we moved up this side, we would have around five or six miles to walk to school. Some mornings it'd be so cold when you get to school you'd nearly freeze. Your hands would be so cold you couldn't hardly rest. You'd have to put them in cold water and your feet would feel like rocks, it was awful. Well, I finally reached the seventh grade, when I was about fifteen. At that time it seems there was no end; we didn't never stop going to school and you never got nowhere seems like. We had the same grades all the time. You know teachers wasn't like they are now. They didn't take up too much time with the children, I don't reckon, then. Look like they didn't learn like they do now. There'd be a gang of children—they only had one room for all the different classes—and they wasn't as strict on the children as they are now.

So we farmed after I was married. Then my husband worked for Mr. W, he was a yardman, and I just stayed in and kept house and raised the children. I used to do domestic work for Mr. W before I got sick with the T. B., and when I got better the doctor told me the best thing to do was to stay home and do my little housework. I had four children, today two are living and two dead. Now right back of the church is where my oldest son lives—he took his daddy's job with Mr. W. My youngest son's building the house right across the road. They come and see me every day.

Just about everybody around here knows everybody. We kind of come up together, raised up together. I call my friends and they call me in the morning to find out how we are. But it's very lonely sometimes, though. My husband's been dead for seventeen years, but my oldest son and his wife stay with me till three years ago and I raised their first baby from a little bitty baby till she was about eight years old. As soon as her mother got able to work she just put the child with me and went to work. When her mother come in, in the evenings, the child don't hardly pay no 'tention to her, it was, "Grandma," all the time. I nursed all my children till they was three years old. Nowadays mothers wants to work all the time, don't want to stop to fool with the babies. 'Course they can always put the babies off on the mother-in-law! My son stay with me till he builded his house out there. It has been about three years. Then my baby son stay with me till he married.

Yes, it's lonely now, but you can always find a little something to do around in the house. And I watch television, the stories mostly; I love them. When I'm not in here, I'm out in the yard doing something. I keep up my yard the best I can. I just grow flowers, I don't have no garden. I gets my vegetables and things from my son. I go to Sunday school and I'm president of the Missionary Society; stay in church practically all of the time, sing in the choir. I was raised up in the church, been a member of the church since I was thirteen. If I don't go I don't feel right through the day.

I can do pretty good through the summer, but when winter come it's pretty hard. I have all my gas bill and light bill and phone bill to pay. It's pretty tight with no more than I get. Way back, I reckon it was in 1940 or '49, people used to string sacks. Do you remember it—these little tobacco bags that most all the colored people use to string? When I quit, at least when the factory went out of business, they sent me a Social Security number. I have been drawing from there. It's very little money but with my little Social Security that I get from my husband and that, why I makes out. That's why I haven't bothered with the food stamps. I feel like other people need them worse than I do.

The biggest thing I dislike about staying here is I don't have no toilet. If I just had me a toilet, I'd be satisfied. There's no running water inside the house. Now I never inquired, but I do know a lady that had a bathroom built and she said hers cost nearly $2,000. That's more than I am able to pay.

The happiest time of my life? Now that is a hard question. To my knowledge I believe the old days was better. I was very happy when I married and I was happy in my childhood too. I guess I have to say when I was married. Then I had somebody to talk to and somebody to take me around—that's why I was happy. The worst thing now is that I cain't get to go nowhere, only when somebody come around and take me. I hate to bother children all the time and I hate to bother my friends. In fact, everybody works around here and it's kinda hard to get anybody. I gets out on Sundays. My children is always off on Sunday and they takes me to church. My son always carries me to the grocery store and to the doctor too, even if he has to get off from work hisself.

Now if I got sick, I have the children to look after me. But I just hope and pray when I gets sick to die, I hope I'll just die. I don't want to be no trouble to nobody. They have children and a family of their own and they has to work. I don't want to bother them from working. I don't know about nursing homes. As far as I'm concerned, I don't think I'd want to go to one. I stayed in the sanitorium for three years (I had T. B. and I had to have my lung out) and I didn't like that too good, so I know I wouldn't like a nursing home. You don't get the treatment that you should get I don't think. They treated me all right because I tried to help myself the best I could, but some of them they couldn't help themselves, they fared common. And I feel like that's the way it would be at the nursing home.

But I'd like to live a long time if I could. It's just some pleasant things in the world I'd like to see: the flowers blooming, the trees, the birds singing, and see the beautiful sunshine and all like that. The Fall of the year always look sad to me. It makes you feel the leaves and things are bidding you goodbye when they begin to fall. Winter makes you feel chilly. In the Spring it begins to liven up again, makes you feel happy. Life is sweet to me.

Ruth Fisher · 71 · "We're living too fast now. We all enjoyed ourselves back then—and we were happy 'cause I don't reckon we knew any better."

Mrs. Fisher, a busy, active, white woman is secretary-treasurer of her small Methodist Church. She has an outgoing personality, and enjoys

visiting her neighbors. A plump woman, of medium height, she was
clad, at the time of our visit, in slacks and a brightly flowered blouse.
Round glasses, resting on a small snub nose, and cropped, gray hair,
accentuate the roundness of her face.

Mrs. Fisher's two-story, wooden house, with its large windows and
narrow front porch running the width of the house, is over seventy
years old, but in good repair. The front door has no lock, and only at
night is latched from the inside. Her house is one of a small cluster of
homes built to accommodate former mill workers.

The mill down here closed down in 1936. My grandmother said
when this mill was making rope and army uniforms, and the Confeder-
ate Army come through here, they didn't even stop and bother anybody.
Grandmother said the army knowed the people were so poor, didn't
have nothing, reason why they didn't bother them.

I worked in the mill when I was twelve years old. The mill didn't
make rope anymore or tobacco sacks like in grandmother's time. I
spinned cotton into thread. I use to work ten hours a day for fifty cents
a day.

There was about thirty or forty families living in this part and
everybody here, men and women, use to work in the mill. When the
mill closed down I went to work in a mill in another town.

I was twenty-one when I married and I had five children. My husband
died when my baby was two-and-a-half years old, and the oldest one
was sixteen. And I remember that I got $71 a month Social Security—
$12 a piece was for each child I think. I raised them five children and
myself on what I got. I stopped working when my husband died.

My Social Security check now is $80 and $161 SSI, $241 in all. But
back then we had a cow, I had chickens, and I had hogs. We raised just
about all we eat. We made out back then when everyone worked for a
dollar a day. You could get a whole lot more then with a dollar than you
can now with five.

We're living too fast now. We all enjoyed ourselves back then. Course
we didn't ever realize there would be a time like it is now. We didn't
have anything, everywhere we went we had to walk, and we were happy
'cause I don't reckon we knew any better. I reckon we get more now
than we've ever had in our lives. But I don't like where it's coming
from. I don't believe in taking middle or poor class of people that's
working and stripping from them that's got families. The managers
take too much off their pay. They're taxing them too high. I just want to
live and do the best I can.

independence

"Don't send me flowers
when I'm dead. I want them now."

Annie Lane · 71 · "Don't send me flowers when I'm dead. I want them now."

Annie Lane, tall and sturdy, her fair complexion shielded from the sun by an old-fashioned sunbonnet, works her land and is proud of it. In very good health, except for deafness, she wears a large hearing aid pinned to her dress. Her favorite recreation is watching the "stories" on television.

Her one-and-a-half story, modestly furnished, six-room house faces the main highway going north from Mill Town to Red Hill. The kitchen has running water, but there is no indoor bathroom. Mrs. Lane spends most of her time outdoors or in her spacious kitchen putting up the produce she harvests.

I was next to the baby in my family. I had to work hard—I was a widow woman's child. I was raised to work. We had to dig our living out of the ground. I quit school when I was in the seventh grade and got married. I was 16 when I married—didn't have a thing in the world but myself and a few clothes. My husband was a farmer, too, so I went right on helping him with the farm. We both worked hard. A farmer never gets rich but we lived a happy life. We were married forty-seven years and worked side-by-side. He'd help me 'round the house and I'd help him in the field. I been alone now seven years and I'm lonely. I miss my husband so much in a lot of things. I didn't have any children, but my niece Lizzie carries me places, and there are neighbors all around me.

In the summer I enjoy getting outdoors and going to work. I forget the house; it almost keeps itself. I do my own mowing of the yard, I work in tobacco, and I have my garden. The garden is sorry this year and late, but I feel thankful I've got what I have. I'll buy me some pinto beans to make out the rest of the way, I reckon, when my other stuff gets low. I made a nice harvest of Irish potatoes. I reckon I made close to twenty bushels. Well, I didn't aim to plant as much as I did. I was out there planting and Bob come. He's a man out here who's awful nice about fixing my garden, plowing it for me. So he was down here fixing the rows and he told me, says, "Go to the house and get your potatoes and we'll plant these potatoes today." So, I come on to the house and got the potatoes, I reckon it was something like three pecks. I didn't cut 'em—just dropped 'em whole. He got through plowing, and he says, "Now, you go to dropping potatoes and I'll finish putting the fertilizer down." So, I didn't pay no attention to him. He kept drilling and I dropped four rows and my potatoes give out. I says, "What in the world we going do now, Bob?" I says, "You've dropped all that fertilizer, now my potatoes done give out." He says, "Go up yonder at mama's." Says, "She's got some and she ain't going plant 'em." So, I went up there and got more than what I had, and I had eight rows. I dug every last one of 'em and tote 'em to the house in a foot tub. They're out yonder in the crib. They're still out there. They're fattening. See, I don't love a potato right by itself, no seasoning. I love butter in 'em. I'm overweight, but I love to eat. I'm trying to lose some of it now, though.

I was raised to work and I still enjoy it. I'll go on working as long as I'm able. When I'm not able, when I get to that, I hope I'll do a big day's work and lay down at night and go to sleep and not wake up.

I tell people. "Don't send me flowers when I'm dead. I want them now." It wouldn't do me two cents worth of good after I'm dead to put me in my grave and put a pile of flowers on me as big as this house. If you've got a flower you want me to have, give it to me while I'm living.

Lizzie Mae Walker · 71 · "I wouldn't want to live my life over the way it was. Saw trees down with a handsaw, and burn old brush piles; no, I wouldn't do that. It's a whole lot easier now."

Fair-skinned and freckled, her snub nose draped by large, rimmed spectacles, Mrs. Walker smiles readily displaying a full set of dentures. Having recently bought herself a gray, curly wig, she decided to wear it for her photograph.

A childless widow living on Social Security, she pays $20 a month rent for the use of a bedroom and kitchen built onto an old uninhab-ited house belonging to her sister-in-law. The house is in poor condi-tion; its sidings of unpainted wood are rotting, and plastic sheets cover the doors and windows. Obviously reluctant to have us visit inside her small bedroom or kitchen, Mrs. Walker seated us outside on the porch, she in a rocking chair, her little black dog at her feet.

I was born right here in this county, made it home all the time. I was happy growing up and I'd rather took to the field anytime than work in the house. Ain't but one thing you were doing in a field, but if you was at the house it's that thing and this thing and another.

It's hard work, field work. We pulled cross-cut saws and sawed down pines nigh big as that oak, and then saw 'em into fine sticks length. Then we'd haul it to the house and roll it up. And we burnt great big brush piles on the new grounds, and we'd cut them roots around them pine stumps and prize 'em out of that piece of land for planting 'bacco or corn. I've growed up in pines. We had hoes in our hands ever since we was 'bout seven or eight years old. The hoe would be too heavy; we'd get a old wore out hoe and put a broomstick handle in it and cut cockleburrs and everything out of the corn. I've worked on the farm all of my life; ain't done a thing but farming.

I wasn't married long. Mama died in 1947 and my husband died in June, 1948. I been a living by myself practically all but 'bout a month right ever since he died, almost thirty years. Didn't never have any children, but I have ten brother and sisters and I have nieces and nephews. I see 'em often. No, I don't get lonesome. If I get confined and have to sit still I'm miserable, so I find something to be a doing and it takes my mind off. Go and pull up some weeds 'round in the yard and knock up some leaves. I sew, I quilt, make my sheets, all of the bed linen, my aprons. But when it's pretty weather I cain't stay in the house; get a notion to go out, I'm gone.

I watch T.V., housewives' programs about love and separating. One was a crying today, had run her husband out last week and he came back today and she says, "Jay, I don't never want to see you again. Don't you put your foot in this house." She says, "I want you to come and get every rag of your clothes tomorrow and I'll be away from home." She wanted to adopt a baby and this man had fires for another woman and she was told about it and man, oh man, she was laying it on him.

I go a heap o' times on a visit and come back. But every trip I make to Mill Town cost me five dollars, unless they've got business selling 'bacco and they'll tell me they had to go anyway and they wouldn't take the money. I use to have to go to the post office in Mill Town every month for my food stamps, but now I can get them at the post office in Ashton.

I get to Mill Town three or four times every two months. My brother carries me, or my nephew does. But my nephew was carried to the hospital this morning. They transferred him a heart.

Now is the happiest life that ever I seen. I ain't never got nobody trying to boss me and tell me what to do. I don't like a boss. My husband didn't do much bossing me 'round; I bossed him 'round. One day he beat the mule 'cause it wouldn't go out to a deep branch to plow his corn and I says, "Look what you caused that mule to do. Break down seven stalks of this pretty corn as pretty as it was." And he says, "Whose farm is this, mine or your'n?" I says, "It just as well be mine; I'm the one that has it to clean up and see after." And he never said another word. Married life was always good for me, but I wouldn't let him have his way over some things if I know I was right. But life is better now. I wouldn't want to live my life over the way it was. Saw trees down with a handsaw, and burn old brush piles . . . no, I wouldn't do that. It's a whole lot easier now.

One thing that would help now is if I had a roomier house so I can place things in it, not like I am here. This house belongs to my sister-in-law, it's her home. I ain't got but two rooms and them is new rooms built on the old house. The old house is just plumb full of everybody's junk 'round here. I'll tell you the truth, my kitchen ain't as big as nothing. I ain't got nowhere in the world to cook and do what I want to do but the middle of the floor. Frigidaire and cabinets and stove, everything a setting 'round and in the way. It's so small.

I don't have nothing in the kitchen that runs water. I run it from the well in a water bucket and tote it in the house. I don't have no washing machine and I don't have nothing to run but electric iron, television, radio, frigidaire and cook stove. Keep a kettle full on the stove to wash dishes. I don't care nothing 'bout a telephone. If I need one, I can step right down here and call. My sister-in-law's got one. I'd rather have running water, and a bathroom in the house. Got neither one. Yeah, I'm warm enough in the winter time. Mary says I know how to burn my oil circulator. But I'm afraid of fire and I cut that heat off at night. I get up of a morning, sometime between three and four o'clock, and light it for the house to warm up, and go back to bed.

If I get sick my sisters will look after me. But if I get sick so I cain't do nothing for myself I'm a going to the rest home. I'll take my Social Security and let them take the check to spend it and keep me. But I'd rather stay here. When you're in somebody else's house you don't know how to do and act. I just as soon for folks to speak what they think about me as to go around, "Pst, pst, pst," whispering. I'm not afraid to live here by myself. I ain't never heard nothing. You know, it was a old man and woman, Elsie Mangum and old man George Mangum live here and she was the one that built these two rooms, and folks ask me have I ever seen Elsie and George or heard 'em. I says, "No, I ain't seen nary one of 'em. I don't look for 'em. I don't listen for 'em. Them folks dead." Folks think that Elsie and George might come and haunt me, but I don't never get scared.

I'm happy as a lark now. My nephew's wife she says, "You ought to live a happy life, Lizzie Mae," and I says, "I do." I says, "When I get mad I ain't got nobody to fuss at and that ends the fuss." When you ain't got nobody to speak to, you cain't fuss.

Lucy Russell · 78 · "We are old and think we don't have to do anything; we use old age as an excuse. I try to discipline myself to never say I am too old to do anything."

Mrs. Russell is a plump, pink-faced lady with snowy, white hair who laughs a great deal. A very pleasant, outgoing person, she is independent, active and energetic, and is still driving her own car.

Her seven-room, white frame house faces on the main road connecting Ashton and Red Hill. A little pond and several large oak trees occupy a small plot behind the house which is fronted by a porch almost hidden by numerous, large, flowering, potted plants. The living room, well furnished and carpeted, leads into a spacious kitchen much used for canning and preserving. The house has indoor plumbing.

I was the oldest of ten. We lived from hand to mouth almost, but we were just as happy as we could be. My parents farmed. My mother would take the babies and sit them under a tree and we'd all work. We'd carry a quilt and a bag of something to eat. Saturday morning we'd take off time from the farm to work around the house and sweep the yard. We had to get dogwood brushes and tie them together to sweep. Twice a year we went to Mill Town in a carriage, driving a horse, to buy winter clothes.

I started teaching when I finished high school at eighteen and taught for ten years, from the first through the seventh grade. I was happy. The first year I made $35 a month for a five month school; I was rich. It was altogether different from what children are now; they respected you. I didn't have much trouble. The second year that I taught I had boys that were older than I was. They had beards, about twenty-one years old, but I never had any trouble with them. I stopped teaching when I married. I was thirty years old. My husband was running a service station in Mill Town and I went to work at the cafeteria in the tobacco factory.

When the depression came, we had forty acres of land that my grandfather left me on the Oxford Highway. In '32, when the depression came, we left Mill Town and moved back out there and lived with my old maid aunt, Betsy. We bought poles to build a log cabin and farmed for six years, then I came up here to the post office as Postmaster, and my husband had a store.

We were laughing yesterday when I said, "I retired sixteen years ago today, and I think, I know, I'm a whole lot older." But I says, "I think I'm a hurting every-once-in-a-while, my arthritis, but I don't think I'm a hurting a bit worse than I was then, if I was to think back." So I should be satisfied, shouldn't I? If I can just keep my eyes so I can read, I'll feel like I'll just get by. The last time I went to Dr. ——, he didn't say a thing about cataracts. He said my glasses was good as any he could give me. But I worry about cataracts.

I have managed well because I think the Lord is blessing me with good health. And then I think there is so many people that give up. And I'm just not one to give up. I have a sister up here at Ashton. She's just folding her arms and going on away, she just sits there. Of course she works around out in the yard, but what I mean is she just thinks that she's old enough to die. We have always been different. When we were young, places she wanted to go I wouldn't want to go, and people she liked I didn't like. I thought about that a lot of times. We were just different. And some people give up and give excuses. They say, "I am getting old enough not to do so and so." We are old and think we don't have to do anything—we use old age as an excuse. I try to discipline myself to never say I am too old to do anything.

I stay busy, I still drive my car, feel like I don't ever get through. If you was to look around you'd see how much I've got started. I still work at the store on Friday most every week. That lets Mrs. C have a day to go to town and get her hair fixed and all like that. And I belong to the church and the United Methodist Women and we have the Home Demonstration Club. I work outdoors a lot with flowers and all that mess, and I knit a lot and read. You'd be surprised at what I like to read. I like best these little Harlequin romances, but if I don't have what I want, I can pick up a farm paper; I read anything. The bad part about it is I'm satisfied right while I am reading it and I know what I am reading, but when I finish reading it, it's gone. I don't guess I concentrate on it.

I don't visit much, never have. That's one reason I go to the store and fill in. I enjoy it. I know I shouldn't stay here by myself and be satisfied. In the winter when the weather's bad, I can stay here for two weeks and never see anybody and it don't bother me a bit. But I know you shouldn't get like that. So I go up there just more to meet people and kind of get out some.

I'll have to say, under the circumstances, I'm happy. I don't have no desire to be running somewhere all the time—you know, traveling all the time—I'm just satisfied at home. I've always been somebody that don't get lonesome. At first it was bad to be alone, I missed my husband. That was it. My daughter and her husband lived here three months after they were married. After they left I think that I thought about my husband more than when they were here, but I've never been one to get lonesome. I know I can sit here for two weeks in the winter and never see anybody, read and knit and I don't get lonesome. And I eat, woman, don't ask me what I eat! I eat all the time. Bacon and eggs, sausage and eggs, anything for breakfast; at lunchtime maybe I'll have a sandwich. I tell you, on Sundays I'll cook a big dinner and then I can always go to the refrigerator and get something to warm up. At night I eat too much, vegetables, anything I can find; I always want some meat, but I don't eat too much sweets.

I try not to worry. I guess you have heard about, "Not to worry about anything that you can't do anything about." If you can't do anything about it, just forget it. I just started doing that.

Elizabeth Thompson · 77 · "The Lord didn't put us in the world to sit and do nothing."

Mrs. Thompson, thin, tall and somewhat stooped, her pale skin pro-tected by an old-fashioned sunbonnet, was working in her yard when we arrived. Her two-story wood house, in good condition, faces the main highway. She appeared dejected. She had nursed sick parents and an ailing husband for many years before they died; her sisters were ailing, she herself had had surgery for cancer, and she was very concerned about her health. But, like many of the elderly in this area, Mrs. Thompson is determined to avoid public assistance. She believes most welfare recipients are undeserving because they haven't tried hard enough to make it on their own.

I work in the garden, I do all my housework, I can, I freeze, and if my neighbors have anything they want me to help them with, I help them. The reason I can manage and others can't is because they don't want to. They just sit and hold out their hands and take. To stay at home on your own you have got to fight. The Lord didn't put us in the world to sit and do nothing. He meant for us to make our own living and do the very best we could. This welfare has ruined our nation. Now if I was eligible for food stamps I wouldn't get them because I don't want people to feel about me like I feel about some of them I know is getting them. I may come to that but things have got to be worse than it is now. I may be too independent. It's a whole lot of them that's getting them food stamps that don't deserve them, and I know it. Food stamps are good if anybody really needs them, but there are so many people on the welfare that don't need to be on it. It is because they don't work, they don't try—young people, black people, white people—everybody can live if they try. If people had to work there wouldn't be this much meanness going on.

Linda Johnson · 73 · "I don't go to church and I don't go to no meetings. I have this here back and leg trouble. I'll hurt so bad 'fore they get ready to preach I won't get nothing out of it."

Mrs. Johnson would rather live alone than with her children because "it is more quiet and peaceful." Through her own resources and help from her children, she manages to take care of herself. Although she has hypertension and a failing heart, and is increasingly troubled with arthritis, Mrs. Johnson's appearance belies her worsening health. Her fair-complexioned face, smooth and unlined, looks far younger than her years. She is a very independent person and speaks her mind plainly.

Visits to Mrs. Johnson, in 1979 and in 1980, showed her memory to be poor, and her physical condition to be deteriorating. On both these occasions we were let into the house by an attendant hired by Mrs. Johnson's family. Mrs. Johnson died of heart failure shortly after admission to the hospital in November, 1980.

Been living alone twenty-some years. I stay here rather than at my son's 'cause I want to live here by myself. It's more quiet and peaceful. If I get to the place I cain't wait on myself, my children told me I could come and live with them if I wanted to. But I've managed all right and I'm not scared to live alone.

I haven't been too well lately, back here about two months ago, I really swelled. And I didn't even know it. Well, it finally got so I couldn't lean nowhere, couldn't get a bit of breath. I reckon it's 'cause I had so much fluid in me. I was admitted to the hospital and they got a whole lot of it off of me.

The first week after I come home, somebody stayed with me every night. One of my daughters-in-law lives right close and she check on me during the day and come and spend the night with me, unless one of my daughters was coming. She fixed me things to eat, and my daughters come and fixed things to eat. I told them it warn't nothing but foolishness to keep running here, staying at night. If I needed anything, I could always reach for the telephone.

My legs and hips has been hurting me now for two months but I do my own housecleaning. I had someone in this morning to help me; the first time I had someone in in a long time. I have the yard mowed when it needs it. When I need to go to the doctor I call my daughter-in-law and she carries me to see him. My daughter-in-law and my son do my grocery shopping.

When I got a letter saying I was eligible to get food stamps my daughter-in-law says, "You are not going to get them." Says, "I'll buy your food if you ain't able to buy them." Says I warn't that bad off. There ain't many that gets them that really needs them. People that gets them darn things is ones that don't try to make nothing. Sounds like begging to me. It makes my daughter-in-law so darn mad to see someone with a cart loaded up with this high price meat and everything pull out the food stamps to pay for them. She comes right on behind and has to pull out money to pay for hers and they are younger than she is.

I pass the time by keeping busy. In the summer I'm working in the yard or shelling, freezing, and so on; in the winter I read a lot. I like mysteries. I sit right here with my feet propped next to that heater and read. Doctor told me to keep 'em propped up when I was sitting. That's what keep 'em from swelling. I have always enjoyed reading, but I never got a chance till after all my kids were married and gone. But I have done my part since. School only went so far as the seventh grade. I stayed in the seventh grade three years. My daddy didn't know I had finished but my mama knowed it, and the teacher didn't care. I could teach better than she could.

I don't go to church and I don't go to no meetings. I have this here back and leg trouble for three or four years and I ain't going to try and sit on them hard benches; I'll hurt so bad 'fore they get ready to preach I won't get nothing out of it. I told them it warn't no point of me taking up the space.

If someone was sick and couldn't wait on himself, they would have to hire someone to stay with them. I don't think nursing homes are what they are cracked up to be. I ain't never been in but two—I was there to see my sister then. I don't think they see after the patients good enough. I know they let them lay there messed up. My daughter's been to visit other folks in the nursing home and they won't even let them clean them up until they eat their supper. You know how good a supper would be laying down there in that stuff. I sure don't want no part of that.

work and poverty

"a strong back and a mule"

Jonah Oakley · 76 · "in the old days all you needed to farm was a strong back and a mule; today you need a college education."

Mr. Oakley, handsome and ruddy faced, short and compact of build, appears to be in excellent health. He is very active, cheerful and alert. Excellent vision and hearing, vigor and stamina, contribute to an appearance and spirit which belie his chronologic age.

The Oakley house is situated in the most fertile and well kept agricultural section of Ashton. The two-story farm house sits high up overlooking a paved road and catches the eye with its fresh coat of yellow paint and red trim. Inside, we saw only the kitchen, spacious, unpretentious and solid, reflecting the owner's personality.

There is nothing on earth that can happen to you that is any worse than losing your companion. But you got to make up your mind whether you want to live on or what do you want to do. Well, really and truly, it was a very long time before I realized I was by myself. It seemed like she just lived on. We had a lot of flowers all around the house here. I was still interested in those flowers and still worked in them just like I did when she was living. It was with the help of the Lord that He didn't let me realize that I was by myself. Had I, I could not have taken it. It just gradually grew on me as the years passed by. That is the way it is. That memory is still there. The things that she lived for—she loved people, worked with them, helped them—I live for them today.

After she passed, I went on up there and got in with Mr. Pickett in the cattle business. I've been in there about twenty years. I am happy there, just as happy as I can be. I love the cattle; I love them to death. I told Mr. Pickett the other day, "I would draw straws to see which I liked the best, you or Mrs. Pickett or the cattle."

I can tell them apart. People don't hardly understand where you got a hundred head of cattle out there, how in the world can you? If one is gone I will know. I can describe any cattle that is gone. I really think that that has carried me along in the world; it has meant so much to me because I was able to do something I wanted to do and like to do. I often think about what my wife used to say. She said that every child was a separate individual in school. You find that in cattle. Without any question, I am sure that everyone of them love me, because strangers can walk in there and they will go off. I can walk in there and they come to me. That's right. And there can be not one in sight, nowhere at all, but I can holler one time—that is all I have to do—you can hear one answer you, and here they are.

I have two children. I have one in Greenville, she has a family of four, and one in New Mexico. The one in Greenville, I see her about every six weeks. And I have a brother that lives near here and I have one that lives in Mill Town. Sisters scattered about every which of way. I see them once a year. Both of my girls are just housewives now. But I educated both of them; they both went to college.

I didn't go past the ninth grade myself. You know, in the old days all you needed to farm was a strong back and a mule; today you need a college education. That is where I come short, but it's one of those things. But Mr. Pickett tells me all the time, "I have never seen anything yet that you couldn't do." I am a mechanic, I am a carpenter, anything comes along, I can do it. I think things happen along through life that helps you out. My wife taught school twenty-two years out of thirty-one years of married life, so she was away. That sort of taught me how to boil water, fry eggs, and things like that. Now I can cook anything, pies, biscuits. I eat out at breakfast and dinner. My night meal is at home.

I get up about five-thirty and by six-thirty I am at my job and it's just about got good and light then. I am on the go all day. Another thing that has been in my favor is I think a lot. I have never worked by whistles in my life; I have always been my own boss. I plan my week's work. When you get up one morning and don't feel as good as you felt the morning before, well then you change your plans just a little bit to take care of yourself along that line.

Now if I got sick I would stay here as long as I could. You know all the blacks in the community are crazy about me, they love me. I am sure that there would be no trouble for me to get somebody to come and help me out. I would rather not go to my children, though I know I'd be welcome a hundred percent. It's just another family, you know. They are my children but they don't belong to me anymore. They belong to them. I've seen some interference with old people coming in and I wouldn't have that to happen for nothing in the world. When little things happen to me I just don't let them know anything about it. Well really, there is not but one way. Like I mentioned a while ago, if somebody will come to your rescue—colored people who it would be—we have some real nice colored people around. I think the worst thing that happens to old people is that some that would love to pick up the little money doing things for other old people don't need that money now because they get Social Security.

I tell you, you have to live so you can live again I think. That has been my motto all through life, to make friends so when you do need something maybe you can call on them. I wouldn't be interested in a rest home. I don't know just what I would work out, but I wouldn't be interested in that. I don't know why, because I have never been to one. I guess it gets monotonous when you stay there a while. With me things don't get monotonous because I am out doing something new every little bit. I guess that's the main thing, that when you get there to old age you have to think about it, but we don't want to. One of these days we are going to get so we can't get around. But I don't have to worry about a nursing home. My children wouldn't stand for that. If they had to slip me out at night they'd get me. The biggest thing that worries me now in getting older is if I should lose my driver's license. That would be bad. I hope that won't happen but it could happen. That is when it would change the picture altogether.

I don't have a doctor. Somebody asked me the other day who my doctor was. I said, "Doctor—who are you talking about?" When I was about thirty years old I had rheumatism so bad I couldn't hardly get about. The doctor kept telling me, "If you want to get rid of the rheumatism, pull your teeth." So that is what I did and the rheumatism is all gone. I had my teeth all taken out when I was thirty years old and a plate put in the same day. I have never been back to the dentist since. I eat corn on the cob, apples, anything.

I tell you one thing, and I wonder if it applies to everyone: I find that the older I get, the less traveling I like to do at night. I can come in at night, pick up the paper and read it, and turn on the T. V., and I am perfectly satisfied and all right until bedtime. Or I'll do some house-cleaning at night. You know, you got to have something to do in order to keep you from going to bed too early. In the winter, I am a great hand to go to dances—Square Dances—onc't or twic't a week. I am crazy about string music; in fact, I have got a violin in there. I make music. I play for many a dance. When the music starts up your feet get going all over the place. That was part of the way I made a living—at night making music. 'Long then they wouldn't give you but a dollar an hour, and you would sit there and play for three or four hours. That would help you out. I do a whole lot of reading. In the summer most anything

I can get hold of. In the winter I go back to my Bible. I read that through two or three times.

I guess my married life when my wife was living was the best time. Like I said, there is nothing on earth that can happen to you that is any worse than losing your companion like that. That is the worst thing in the world. But you got to work out that problem where you will be the most happiest in living alone.

My hobby is work. I don't fish, I don't hunt. I spend the most of my leisure time round the cattle. That is the only way you can do and get them to know you so you can handle them. I had a cow that had got cripple, and I had to get her up through three pastures. I wondered just how I was going to do that, but I reckon in about forty minutes I had her up following me. I think I will keep working with cattle. It is something I like very much. If I just quit I might get old. I know of several people that have retired and they are very much upset, dissatisfied. I guess maybe I better hang on. I don't want to get old.

George Ross · 83 · "It took all the money I had to pay the doctors."

An erect, young-looking white octogenarian, with aquiline nose, high forehead and thinning white hair, George Ross is a jovial man. He lives in a small frame house consisting of a living room, bedroom, kitchen and screened back porch. His five-acre lot also contains his youngest daughter's mobile home—his daughter visits him daily. His house is heated by two wood-burning stoves which he also uses for cooking because he finds it too expensive to use his electric stove. The kitchen has plumbing, but there is no hot water heater, nor indoor bath and toilet.

Mr. Ross enjoys his robust health, his daily walk, the food he is accustomed to eating, a drink of good liquor, and congenial company. Independent and seemingly self-sufficient, he lives on Social Security and refuses to get food stamps because "maybe somebody need them worst than I do; let them have them. The less that asks, that gives the others a better chance what ain't got it." Unlike most of his neighbors and friends, he has no church membership.

I ain't got no education. Went through two grades, first and second; that's as far as I got. When I got big enough to do anything on the farm, I stayed home from school and worked. I was happy; I didn't know nothing else but work on the farm.

My daddy rented from pretty big people. They had a farm and a sawmill 'bout eight or ten miles from home. We was tending the crop on halves. When I don't have a job on the farm I work for the man at the sawmill. We'd go on a Monday morning and stay till Saturday. I slept many a night with my shoes on, slept on the floor in a shack with a fireplace, and the colored folk slept in the shed. We eat on a great big box; a colored man done the cooking, cooked great big hoe cakes in the pan, fry meat, molasses and bread. Our mules had a trough nailed up outside. We get up in the morning, the colored fellow feed the mules, and we go to work. Haul the lumber, drive the mules, eat supper nine, ten o'clock. We don't have them times now.

I never did join no church. All of them churches don't lie, but everyone's different, you know. I have said church people will preach to you things to do that's right and they'll turn 'round and do something I don't care to do. The worst treatment I had was from a good church-man. I says, "Why do some people think you have to go to church every Sunday?" They says, "Well, to show people how you live." I says, "Well, how do they live the other six days?"

After I got married I still farmed on halves, and when I got in shape I bought me two mules and worked to pay for them. My wife was a good woman, kept house, did the cooking, everything. When she was living I'd go to the house from working and she'd have a great big bowl of snaps cooked, a big slice of fat meat laying on it, some cornbread, buttermilk. That's the way I come up way back yonder.

My wife and I, we had as good a life as any of the rest of them; we got along good, me and her. We was broke when we married, I was twenty-one, she was nineteen, neither one had nothing, and what we got we had to work for. She took care of me and help me all she could, went to the field and help me. When the children got old enough they went to school. But when we had to put in our tobacco they all come out of school and help me put the tobacco in, help me save the tobacco crop. And the corn I'd pull it down and haul it up in a great long pile and have a corn shucking. My wife would cook and the neighbor women would come in and help her cook. Same thing when we had a hog killing. My wife and my mommy and the neighbors be over helping me clean up, get the lard fixed, dry the sausage, get the meat all cut up and salted down in the smokehouse. I get a colored woman to come help my wife, and they cook dinner for all of us.

When my children was growing up a little, just going to school, me and her we never went to town but onc't or twic't a year. We went in the fall selling tobacco and she'd buy clothes and shoes for them children to go to school on. And next spring—she go to church—she get their Sunday dresses and shoes to wear for Sunday. And she raised a bunch of chickens. 'Bout every two weeks we carry them to the store and trade them out for sugar, coffee, some cloth to make a dress. She done her sewing at home for all them kids. She carried her housework like she want to, and me my outside work like I want to, and that's the way we lived. We lived together fifty-one or fifty-two years.

After my wife died, I sold my mules, my cow, my hog. I said, "I ain't got nobody with me," and I quit farming. I rented all my life, but when I quit farming I bought this little place. I couldn't buy a farm; all I got here is five acres.

Right now it's kind of lonesome a whole lot of the time. I reckon that's the hardest thing, sitting by yourself. A lot of nights I'm here by myself and I go to bed too soon. The later I go to bed, the better I can sleep.

Must have been 'bout two years or more that I quit driving, after I had my accident and broke my arm. But nobody don't have to come here and carry me to the store. I walk up yonder 'bout half a mile; I hardly miss a day. Got to do something for exercise. I get up in the morning, eat breakfast, sit here a while, get some wood that need splitting, split that up and put it on the porch, walk 'round here, mess 'round, walk up to the store and get me a pepsi-cola and come back, fry me some eggs and sausage, drink my coffee. I ain't never give up doing my little jobs at the house, clean my house, wash my clothes, mow my lawn. The doctor told me not to mow my lawn no more but I don't want snakes slipping in my door. I have a little garden and I give it to them that ain't got no garden and no way of having one. I give it away and I don't give it away neither; they cook a whole lot of it and bring some to me. Miss Watson, me and her was in the first grade together, she cooked me one of the prettiest dinners for Christmas you ever saw.

I got a sister [Rose Chambers] down here; me and her is twins. She don't get 'bout like I do. I told her she didn't get 'bout enough. She goes bent over. You can give over and get all hump shoulders, you cain't straighten up I reckon. You got to try to keep yourself up if you can. I get 'round. My neighbors go by and see me in the yard. If they don't see me messing 'round they come over. If you ain't got no friends you in bad shape.

What I'm trying to do is to have enough money to get me something to eat, and if I have to go to a doctor have money to pay him. My Social Security is all I got.

The last time I went to the hospital I couldn't make no water for about a week. This boy that married my daughter was telling me how good his doctor was and his price warn't so bad, so he carried me down there to the hospital that his doctor was at.

The doctor said, "I'll wait on you, I'll tend to you." He done all that but then had two more doctors coming in checking me all over everywhere and I didn't need 'em. I told 'em I didn't need that.

They operated on me a few days after that. I sat back just near 'bout asleep, no pain, and I could see 'em working, but I couldn't understand a word from nobody. I couldn't feel a thing and I don't know what they done.

The doctor seemed good to me and I had good nurses, colored and white, just as good as you could ask for. I had a room to myself and a big television. I didn't find but one fault of being down there. What they fixed to eat, I just didn't like the taste, it ain't cooked right, ain't seasoned, it didn't suit me. But they give me plenty of that food and drinks, them girls just pass it out to me.

After a few days I was getting better and better and my doctor come to see me and them other two doctors did too. My doctor said, "Now I'm going to turn you a loose and I want you to go home, and I want you to leave that lawnmower alone. Don't you fool with that thing. And I don't want you to lay around on the bed and sleep. I want you to eat anything you want and all you want and drink anything you want and all you want, and get around, stir about." "Well," I said, "Doctor you couldn't turned me a loose no better satisfied." I never could be still all the time.

The next time I was at the hospital was after a month when I went for a check-up. My doctor come and checked me out and he said, "Mr. Ross, you're getting on good." I said, "Well, I feel alright and if I feel like I do now I won't never have to come back to another hospital." He said, "You'd better. I want you to come back here in two months."

Then it come to me, I ought to say this. "Doctor, what 'bout my hospital, doctor bill down here?" I didn't want to stay out and not say nothing to him. It wouldn't be right, look kind of tricky to me to do that. I wanted it settled up, and let him know it.

"Well," he says, "Come on." We went out that room, down that little hall, all the way into another room, and there was two women in there just wrapped up with papers at work. He talked with one of 'em and come back and says it'll be nine hundred and some dollars. I pulled out ten one hundred dollar bills and give him and he brought me back forty, and then I went to the office and got me a receipt. The nurse there say, "Now, Mr. Ross, you watch your mailbox, you're going to get a check [Medicare reimbursement]." I says, "Well, I'll do it, I live right at my mailbox and I'll phone the post office and I'll watch it."

The next day my check come for $665. Anyhow, first thing you know I got a dun from one of them extra two doctors that examined me! Took 'bout nearly $200 back. Then here comes a bill from the other one! Now what good did that check do me? How much good is it if I give you something and then somebody else come and take it away? I couldn't see where it was much help to me.

I come back home and I had to live, had to have clothes, a light bill to pay and all such as that, insurance what I had to have, and high as stuff is it cost you something don't it? And I said, and I believe I told you all, "I never expect to go to that hospital no more." Because if they cain't tell you the truth, you get enough of a thing one time, don't you? They ought to knowed better than that after I told him I don't need them other two doctors.

If you got me doing a job of work for you and I come in there and do it and then drag in somebody else and sticking their name on it, now what is that? Now, it runs in my mind them doctors that come in there, they may be what you'd call old junky people somewhere, they got no job, probably cain't get nary one, and he likes 'em and he'll take 'em in. It could work that way; it runs in my head that way. I cain't help from wonder, and the older I get, the more I think, the more I study and think 'bout it, I believe a lot of it is true.

No, I ain't never been back to the hospital. I walked up here to the store last week, and I started 'cross the railroad and somebody drove up behind me on a pickup. They stopped beside me and I seen it was my main doctor. He wanted to know how I was getting on and all like of that. He owns a farm back here and he and his wife was going fishing down there. I told him I was getting 'long good. I didn't tell him a thing in the world; I ought to, but I didn't tell him nothing.

I'll tell you, the first time I ever had to go to a doctor I was eighty years old when I got my arm broke, and I didn't have but one doctor. And the next time I had a puncture [hernia], and I went to the hospital for that and I hadn't know but one doctor. And then when I went down to Mill Town General Hospital, that's when I had all them other two doctors coming in. I tell you, I want one doctor and that's enough. One doctor.

Let me tell you. You women here now, you housekeeping ain't you, you all have little jobs of work? Well, if you hire somebody, somebody comes to you and wants a job and you take 'em, you're paying him for it, you don't pull somebody else in and have to pay them, do you? Do you? Now I'm not holding nothing 'gainst this doctor because I reckon he done all he could, but he could have had something to do with them two a coming in there, and taking more of my money. Now that's right, isn't it?

A poor man like I am cain't go the hospital and come back home and live. He's got to hire his wood cut and pay his oil for the lawnmower. It took all the money I had to pay the doctors.

Louis Matthews · 76 · "Lord, if people had to work now like they did then, I don't know what they'd do."

Louis Matthews, his deeply lined, weather-beaten face stained with tobacco juice, smiles and laughs readily, displaying many missing and carious teeth. His wiry body clothed in overalls, he appears to be always active, alert, and in good health despite his bad teeth and increasing deafness. Always busy, on two visits we found him in the tobacco fields. During breaks we interviewed and photographed him.

His two-room, deteriorating frame house needs painting and repairing but is kept clean and neat by his youngest daughter. There is no indoor plumbing; Mr. Matthews gets his water from a neighbor's well and has what he calls an old-timey outhouse.

I reckon when I was growing up, that's 'bout the happiest time. When I stayed at home, 'fore my daddy died, we all was getting up big enough to help him farm and we didn't have a thing in the world to worry 'bout. I'd say I started to working when I was 'bout eight or nine years old, most anything that come to hand that I could do, and I plowed. We use to break all the land in the fall of the year. Do all the fall plowing with mules and horses. Back then people'd do a whole lot of clearing up new ground. Cut the wood and haul the wood off and tear the land up, and that was our home near 'bout through the winter, new ground, clean up. Had to get the briar patch off in the wintertime. Briars as high as this jalousie here, be so thick you have to get down at the ground and kind of work your way in there to cut it, strip 'em up. Lord, if people had to work now like they did then, I don't know what they'd do. Now they got tractors, they don't ax the briar patch, just go right on through it.

We got to go to school in the winter, go every chance we could. Log cabin school house, I had 'bout eight years of schooling, I reckon.

Got married in 1922, and stayed married more than fifty years. Yes, ma'am, we got along just fine, we got along awfully good. I had a mighty good wife. She been dead, now, 'bout four years. Now when she died everyone of my children says, "Now, Daddy, you come live with us." I says, "I ain't going nowhere." I says, "I'm gonna stay right on here, long as I can." And so they says, "Well if that's what you want to do it's all right." Look like I'm better satisfied here than anywhere else. And they're scattered 'bout not too much. Two of my four children lives close by. Everyone of 'em works public work, they ain't none of 'em farmed. Now my youngest daughter, she comes every Sunday that comes, brings dinner and we all have dinner here together, and she does my washing and she comes onc't during the week and cleans up. She's mighty good to me. Well all of 'em is as far as that goes. My daughter goes to the grocery store onc't a week to do her grocery shopping, and while she's buying she'll get me mine too. 'Cause you can get it a little bit cheaper'n you can at these country stores.

I've been blessed with right good health. Comes from hard work I reckon. Don't know of nothing else, 'cause that's what I've been use to all my life is hard work. I don't drink, I don't smoke, I don't dip, but I chew; I got to have a chew of tobacco. I eat mostly eggs since my wife died. That's something I don't believe I'd ever get tired of, two fried eggs at morning and four boiled eggs at night. I'll eat a snack at noon maybe, from the grocery store; maybe I'll get me a hamburger or something like that. Nowadays, after I have breakfast of a morning, I get out in the fresh air and stir around. I walk 'bout four miles a day, just 'round different places on the farm.

I went down here to the clinic last summer. That's something I hardly ever do. My head got stopped up and I couldn't hear anything, hardly. They washed my head out and I declare, I come back—we was putting in tobacco—and I went back to the barn and started the machine up, and I never heard such a fuss in my life. I says, "Good gracious alive, this here thing's making a whole lot more fuss that it was."

I hardly ever get sick; don't take a thing but one-a-day vitamin, onc't a day. The clinic want my teeth all pulled out, says it'd be a free job. They says, "We cain't put you in any false teeth, but we will pull them." I tell you right now, this here toothache is terrible.

I think the old days was better than now. People was different back when I was growing up than now. You never heard tell of any killings 'less you's way yonder somewheres. Now, kill one another right in your backyard what you might say, and people, they just want you to go along with it. Now my grandchild, eighteen years old, got killed here 'bout three months ago. Man just shot him, he took a gun and shot him. Jack asked me the other day, says, "Ain't you scared to stay here by yourself?" I says, "Good gracious alive, no. Why, the neighbors live right out there, anything happens I can holler." If they ain't seen me, they come to see 'bout me.

See, I still farm. I help the others mostly. I still work in tobacco, and I been a helping a fellow. Treating plant beds for another year, putting gas on 'em and putting plastic covers over 'em; next spring they come and take 'em plastics off and sow the beds. There's all the time something to do. Now in cold, bad weather I sit by the fire. I don't get out too much anymore when it's snow on the ground or raining or bad weather. I have to stay in to try to take care of myself to keep colds off, flu. Tobacco season's the onlyest time I make any money. Others times I just have what you might say, accommodations. I hear a lot of 'em say they couldn't make it from one month till the other on what they was a getting, but I try to; I ain't never put in for no raise or nothing like that. I just take what they hand me and try to make it. I get by with it, and my Social Security check, $94.70 a month.

John Taylor · 73 · "What would make life easier? I would like to have something different to eat once in a while."

Mr. Taylor, an extremely thin, very shy white man, covers his mouth with his hand and turns his face away while answering questions. He lives rent-free in a dilapidated log cabin belonging to a neighboring farmer. The one-room house has no ceiling and only rudimentary furnishings: a bed, a cupboard with a curtain for his clothes, and two chairs. His cook stove is a two-burner hot plate and he has a wood-burning stove for heating. He has no telephone and no indoor plumbing; he carries his water from a well across the street. He does not own a television or a radio, the house is not very clean, and in general it is one of the poorest houses that we visited. Mr. Taylor draws the minimal Social Security pension, is not on Medicaid, and does not get food stamps.

I made out pretty good this winter. It took right much wood in there. I kept a fire all night when it was real cold. I buy my wood. I got some on the place but by the time I get it cut. . . . See, I ain't go no way to cut it and haul it, and it don't cost no more for somebody else to cut it and deliver it. Of course they charge me more now than they used to.

I been doing pretty good. Still taking medicine, heart pills and fluid pills, and then I take this packaged medicine in orange juice. I keep my medicine checked, and then if it's too low I have to always try to keep some ahead.

I reckon if I had to go to a nursing home I'd have to like it. But I'd rather be home. I reckon I like living out here because I was born in this county and raised out here.

My parents used to farm and I started working on the farm when I was eight years old. My sister and brother are both dead and my mother and father are gone too. I'm not married; I just didn't care nothing about it. I pass the time now by doing a little work; I go and help Mrs. Briggs some in the store, maybe mow her yard. I cain't take no regular jobs now. I get out and walk a whole lot—walking gives me a lot of pleasure. I cain't sit around long. I go to town once in a while—usually catch a way—go shopping there. I go to a cafe and eat my lunch and then I go back home.

I don't cook much, hardly ever. It's not hard for me to cook, not if I get my mind on down to it, but I usually eat out. I eat up here to the store a whole lot and go into town and eat at the cafes. What would make life easier? I would like to have something different to eat once in a while.

Following amputation of both his legs, necessitated by blockage of his blood vessels and subsequent gangrene, Mr. Taylor, who told us, "I reckon if I had to go to a nursing home I'd have to like it," has spent the last two years in Greenwood Rest Home.

We visited him there. He remains a solitary person, staying mostly in his own room, though he joins the group occasionally. The rest home owner appears to be genuinely concerned about his welfare and takes good care of him.

Bill Parrish · 68 · "Then when I was in the second grade, mama took me out o' school and put me to work for twenty cents a day."

His shoulders stooped, his clothes unkempt, Mr. Parrish's eyes twinkled and a mischievous look brightened his ebony-black, aging face as he noted our absorption in his story.

The screen door of his small frame house is torn, the house and grounds neglected and littered. Furnishings are shabby and meager. At the time of our first visit a wood stove was burning in the living room even though it was a very hot day. In the kitchen empty beer cans were strewn around. Although Mr. Parrish owns a big freezer, it was empty at the time of our visit.

I ought not to say it, but I had a sorry daddy. I wouldn't walk in his footsteps for nothing. He warn't worth nothing. Mama was scared o' him. He cut a man, mortgaged everything he had, and went away from here to Columbus, Ohio. The only time I left Ashton—and far as I ever been in my life was Columbus, Ohio—when I was told my daddy was dead and I went up there. I didn't have no money to ride in the pretty cars; I had to ride in the baggage car and the conductor was so mean. I had to spend my money to put my daddy away.

When he left my mama I warn't but six years old, and he had two children under me. So my mama seed after us, 'cause we didn't know how to do any plowing. We had a horse and a mule; she say how much she want us to plow every day. Sometimes our horse'd give out and our old mule just couldn't do, he just walk away. He had sense, Old Tom, he'd get out there and halfway run 'bout half the day and then give out the rest of the day.

Then when I was in the second grade, mama took me out o' school and put me to work for twenty cents a day for Mr. D. I'd plow, get out there when the sun riz. I was nine years old when I started working for him. I remember that good, just as good as I remember anything. Nine years old and I had to walk a mile and a half to work on Monday morning then I stayed all week. The rule was then you work till Saturday dinner and come home.

Mama house cleaned; so many folks she work for. She would cook us fritters. Take you a big spoon and stir that dough up and spread with blackstrap molasses. We plant a plenty cane to make a barrel of molasses and that last us a long time.

Now I don't smoke. My mama whipped me when I was thirteen years old and I ain't had a cigarette in my mouth since. She find me and say, "Sitting out there behind my chimney there, slipping away to smoke, you hip-head rascal you. I try my best to kill you." She didn't get no chance to whip me no more 'bout no cigarette. And I didn't drink when my mama was living. I started that up since she's dead.

After I stop working for Mr. D I work for the people built this dam out here. We was grading the road. Mr. E had the wheelers [*large scoops for dredging dirt, mounted on wheels and dragged by mules*] to haul the dirts 'round. I work there 'bout a year. And then when I quit the wheeler camp I work on the dam for two years. Then I went to the railroad and stayed the balance of my days till I retired. That's right. Put in cross ties and everything, changed out rails.

I was twenty-two when I got married. My wife had T. B. 'fore we married. I had eight children, five dead and three living. Three died from meningitis, doctor say; I got so much miseries I don't know what the others die from. They took one baby away from my wife in the hospital [miscarriage]; that cost me 'bout $3000. Dr. Walters, she the doctor would go 'round you know [public health physician], she stop my wife sleeping with me. My wife slept in that room and I slept in this one. Dr. Walters say she put the law on me if she catch me sleeping with my wife. They put my wife in Kane Hospital [T. B. sanatorium] for three years 'fore she come back home. It's been 'bout four years that my wife been left me. She say she don't understand the country no more— she's townsfolk. The only thing I know she left me 'cause she want to live in town where we got a daughter live right next door to her now.

I retired two years now but I still works 'round. I cut grass for the white folks, cut 'em a walkway in the snow. When I ain't working I sit on my porch and watch the traffic pass. Sometimes I go down to the boathouse and sit and listen to the white folks talk. I don't make talk when they talk; I be quiet. When they say something embarrass, something wrong that I think I know better than that, I don't say nothing. I don't meddle in they talk. I don't fish on Sundays. My mama wouldn't let me 'cause that's a bad habit. And if anybody in the world violate their mama's rules, I don't know what to think of 'em. I go to church sometimes but it's far to walk. They took my driving license. Say I was under the 'fluence. I got with the wrong gang, had one, and the law caught me. The game warden, he the one that arrested me. If I'd knowed it was the game warden I'd have tried to outrun him and got back home. They been having my license 'bout four years.

If I got so I cain't look after myself I wouldn't want to go to a nursing home. They're pretty bad. There was this Lassiter man, he died there. He don't have nobody to take care of him. I don't say they treat 'em bad, but they don't pay 'em no 'tention at all. Down here at Pleasant Rest, where Fred Lassiter was, I went down there to see him. He's laying in the bed, no cover on him. I say, "Where's the cover he's suppose to have?" I reckon they had to put 'em in the laundry. They wasn't as clean like in the hospital where they dress your bed onc't a day.

I think what old people need to keep 'em from going to nursing homes is a good quiet seventy year old woman to stay with 'em. I think while you living good, and you got your health and strength, and you got plenty of friends, you got to pick out somebody to hold you up. 'Cause if you don't, when you get to walking with a stick and somebody see you coming up the road there, they come in here and shut the door.

I don't want to get married again. Sometimes everybody act like they be white folks trying to teach me. They say, "Cain't you get another woman to marry you, to stay with you?" I say, "No, I done separated the wheat from the chaff onc't; I ain't going to try it over again." If I was sick my sister'd take care of me. This Clyde Williams, worked on the railroad years ago, he say he don't need no woman in the world to do nothing but wash and cook for him. He say if you got one to cook for you when you get his age, that's all you ought to need.

I gets lonesome sometimes but right now is my best time in my life I ever had, right now. I ain't got no children crying to keep me woke all night, I ain't got nobody to bother me right now, and my money check comes in the mailbox.

I don't reckon I ever want to live somewhere else. I was throwed 'round so much when I had to work. When I was working my boss he'd call me up, "You got to go to Halifax. You got to go to South Boston. What time do you think you can get here?" I'd say, "I'm on my way right now." I don't have to go through with that now. Bill Parrish don't have to go through with that now. When I lay down, I just lay down all night if I want to. People in this world just wants too much and ain't satisfied with what God Almighty give 'em. I'm satisfied if my check come. I'm a retired man and my check come and it ain't much, but I'm satisfied.

Now suppose I warn't getting that little check. My children'd hate to see me coming and glad to see me leave. But now I go 'round to some o' 'em and they're glad to see me, and that's the only understanding I got in this world.

Walter Jordan · 71 · "Well, I do pretty good by being stingy, as they call me."

Mr. Jordan, an elderly black man, pays only $4 a month rent for his two-room log cabin. The cabin is lined with cardboard from discarded packing cases. His sleeping / living area is furnished with a bed, chair and small table supporting a television and a radio, and is heated with an oil circulator. The only window in this room is boarded up against the cold and is lit by a single, naked light bulb hanging crookedly from the ceiling. The kitchen has a wood stove, in need of repair, a table, chair, and old refrigerator. Wiring for electricity is exposed. Many open and discarded cans litter the cabin, and Mr. Jordan's clothes hang on nails knocked into the walls. There is no indoor running water and no outside privy.

We saw a well-kept green, four door Buick sedan parked near the cabin. Mr. Jordan had bought the car second-hand in 1973, with help from his brother.

During the entire interview, Mr. Jordan, who has no teeth, was chewing a plug of tobacco. Some years later the acquisition of a set of dentures transformed Mr. Jordan into a handsome man.

I just got in the fourth grade and they took me out and put me to work on the farm. I worked on the farm off and on till it pay so little we couldn't farm any. I worked at the sawmill and government work [WPA] all the time after that. I started to work at the sawmill before I was twenty and I work at the sawmill off and on 'bout six years in and out, but I don't know exactly when I quit. When I married I went to work on the railroad putting in ties and cutting grass, cleaning out ditches. And then they laid me off from the railroad, so I went back to farming again.

If I'd knowed I could o' went back out there on the railroad I wouldn't o' went to farming, I'd o' went back out there; but I didn't know it was just a lay-off, I just thought I was finished and off for good.

So I was tenant farming Martin Crawford's land; I ain't worked with him but one year. That's fore I married. Well, I farmed again, me and my wife, at different one's farms till 1950. My wife, she had had an operation and she couldn't stand the sun much after that, so I just throwed up farming again. Course I like farming and I'd rather to do it than to do anything else.

I just went back to public work again. I was working for a construction company, building houses and things like that. I stayed there till I got cut off there, then I went down here on Pine Road working for a tire company. Then they got to calling people, wanting people at the tobacco factory. My nephew, he was working up there and he told me I could get a job there till the green season give out. Then I had to get me a job somewhere else wherever I can get one at. But every year, though, whenever they'd call me back, I'd quit where I was at and go back to the tobacco factory. Finally, when they had that cut off, my wife told me, "Well, you don't work at the factory but 'bout two, three, or four months; they cut it off and then you have to get you a job wheresomes you can. Now whenever you get a job you ought to stay there. I wouldn't go back there no more." But I wouldn't take her advice.

I was working with a construction company when I got a letter, a registered letter from the tobacco factory. So I went on down to an office there at the factory and a lady says, "Yeah, we got a opening for you, a year-round job." That's just what I wanted. She says, "Well, can you be here Monday morning at seven o'clock?" I told her, "Yes, ma'am." So I worked there for ten years till I retired, year-round job on the cigarette side, but I didn't work long enough to draw a pension from there. I just get Social Security, 'bout $150 some a month.

Well, I do pretty good, by being stingy, as they call me. Some of 'em tried to get me to put in so I could get food stamps, but I said, "Well, I ain't going run into that, not if I can help it." Yeah. Might be some difficulty or something or other.

My brother, the one in Connecticut, put in that telephone for me. I ain't never been no hand at writing. When he left here he put that in so he could call and we liable to call him. I call 'bout onc't a month. If it was for me a having this put in here, it wouldn't never been in here.

I don't want to put water in here 'cause it'd be limestone water and I don't care for limestone water, cain't drink it. I get my water up here where the guy that I was helping in tobacco live. Ain't far, right up there going up the hill. There's nowhere out here to put a toilet unless it would be standing full of water all the time. I use hers [Georgia Brown, his landlady] up there whenever I choose to. If I don't, I go to the woods.

I don't want another job. I work for a guy some few days, help him putting in tobacco, but other than that, that's all I do. After he has his tobacco housed, nothing to do. To tell you the truth 'bout it, I ain't the man to work on a regular job like I used to.

What I do now is get up in the morning and cook and eat and fix up and do everything and sit 'round till 'bout twelve o'clock. Sometimes I leave before then, and then sometimes I stay here all day. I go visiting to a lot of different one's houses. If I leave here about twelve o'clock I'll stay away till 'bout the middle of the evening. I go down sometimes to visit with my nephew. He loves for me to be with him — go 'round with him, have a little fun — laugh and talk and go 'round to different one's houses. Then in the summertime when I ain't doing nothing, I go up and sit 'round the store. I watch television 'bout every night. I like Archie Bunker, hear him cut the fool. And I go to church.

What's the worst thing 'bout living alone? I ain't found nothing, except it gets lonely. Well, thing of it is, I's doing all right for an old man. I can get 'bout; I'm not handicapped or nothing. I did break my leg, but it's all right now. After I retired from out there, from the tobacco factory, one Christmas Eve I was down to my nephew's. It was raining that night and it was freezing. I went outdoors, got out on the porch and just couldn't stop, I just kept on, and I kind o' slipped up. I couldn't get up and my foot's sore. It were a couple o' weeks before I went to the hospital to see a doctor with it. I thought it was just sprained. They took and examined me and told me, say, "Well, it's not broke, it's fractured." Well, I put it to the same thing, broke is fractured, and they put it in a cast and I had to stay off o' it a long time. My brother-in-law carried me to his house and I stayed up there till the cast got took off.

I don't recall nothing that would make my life no better, I don't reckon. Some of 'em tell me, "Why don't you get married, get you a wife?" I says, "Far as that's concerned, I won't get one like I had, like the first one. Ain't nary one like her." So I says, "Long as I'm going on now I can go to bed when I get ready, get up when I get ready, or go where I want to and come when I get ready, and I ain't having no head-aches now." I says, "I figure if I marry another woman I'll have a head-ache." And I don't want that.

James Poole · 79 · "My parents farmed other people's farms all their lives by renting on halves or three-fourths. I started helping from when I was 'bout four or five years old."

Mr. Poole is over six feet tall, erect and trim. His ebony face is without a wrinkle and his general appearance is that of a man in his fifties. Except for a slight hearing loss and an occasional arthritic ache, he is apparently in excellent health. Despite his lack of schooling he is remarkably well spoken.

Mr. Poole's small frame house sits at the end of a narrow dirt road off the main road, and is surrounded by large trees. Loose, drab material covers the living room sofa and arm chair. Heat is provided by a wood stove in the living room; a wood stove in the kitchen is used for cooking. Water in the kitchen is pumped from a well, and there is no indoor bath or toilet. The small kitchen and smaller back porch are cluttered with buckets, old plastic containers filled with water, cooking utensils, and gardening tools. Inside and out the condition of the house is deteriorating.

I never married; I just went on like I was. One thing, I had my mother to see after, and all the rest of the children married and left. I didn't feel like it would be the right thing for me to leave her. She died in '45 when she was about eighty-eight. Since then, one or two of my sisters stayed here part of the time. My oldest sister, she stayed here until her health went bad and she died. My next oldest sister, she stayed here a while and she left. So I have been here ever since about 1950, twenty-five some years.

My parents farmed other people's farms all their life by renting on halves or three-fourths. I started helping from when I was about four or five years old. I just done whatever a child could do, chopping with a hoe and something like that until I got big enough to plow a mule. I didn't have no daddy to raise me; my father and mother separated years ago when I was a baby.

When I was of school age, the school was about seven or eight miles from us. We didn't have sufficient things to wear to go that far in the cold, so I didn't go to school. All the rest went, but I didn't go at that time. I was the eldest. I learned to spell a little bit, and count figures a little bit, and things like that, but I cain't write. I can print my name but I cain't write it.

So I farmed ever since I been big enough up until now. I farmed up until last year. I think that it is a good thing if you able: it keeps you in action. I feel like, a person as long as his health is sufficient for him to get around and do things, I think it is a fine thing for him to do as long as he's able. This year I got to the place I thought that the tobacco was more than I could tend. I had to go through a whole lot to get it housed. Then the expense of it got so high, it wasn't worth it. Now I just hang around and do little things that need to be done. I go to church most every Sunday. I use to walk all the time but now I am getting old and I don't walk as much as I use to. I get the lady that lives up on the hill; they have to go out to church the same route that I do. If they don't, I get somebody else; I have a lot of friends.

Yes, I have right smart many friends around here. I've always tried to use myself in a way so that I would gain friends rather than lose friends. I raised a bunch of children too. I don't have any of my own; these are my nieces and nephews. I raised more than a dozen, and they were living here with me when I raised them. Whenever I need to send to the grocery store I call some of them to come and bring me.

Just as long as I am able to do for myself I would like to remain on like I is. Of course I may have to go, I don't know. My health is very good; I have a little sinus headache, but other than that I am doing pretty good. My Social Security isn't very big, less than $100 a month. A person has to strain to live with that. Half of that goes to bills, and a person still have to live, but I make out, though I don't have no money to spare. My light bill is about $10 and my water bill run something like that. I use wood for heating and cooking.

Yes, it would make it a lot better if I had a bathroom. A bathroom would make it easier for people to stay by themselves. Then too, maybe if old people wasn't able to get wood or make fires, maybe arrangements could be made to get a little oil or heat. I think when a person get so they cain't wait on themselves, some arrangements could be made. Lots of people is not got the convenience and such things for to take care of older people like they have at the nursing home. They fixed for their business.

If I got sick, some of the children I raised would look after me regardless of what happen. In case they wasn't in [financial] shape as much as they would want to, I'd prefer going to the nursing home, a place where I would be seed after. I have a sister in a nursing home and she says she getting on pretty good. She's kind of mental minded, cain't remember things good. Well, it seems as if they taking right good care of her. They keep her clean and every time I go to see her she seems to be doing okay. I think it's a fine place—whenever your health get so that you need to go—I think that's the place for you.

The happiest time of my life has been when I was thirty-five up until now. The time before that I didn't see things as well as I did after I got grown. Then I could see that it was necessary to sort of take care of myself and go to looking out for a better life, like going to church, joining the church, 'tending the service, and things like that. I wasn't interested before that. The change came from just a feeling I had, that I wasn't living according to like I should. One thing now is that I'm just glad that I live this good number of years, and I'm proud of my health. I think its a blessing to have some older people around to tell younger folks about old times and experience and be a help to them. If all the older people would die out the younger people wouldn't have the knowledge unless it's something they read.

Sarah Allen · 65 · "I don't chew tobacco, I don't smoke, and I don't dip."

Of medium height and slight build, always wearing slacks, Mrs. Allen, her fair skin weathered from constant outdoor activity, is hyperactive, hardly sitting still even during relaxed conversations.

She lives in a one-and-a-half story, 100-year-old, white frame farmhouse. The original log walls have long since been covered over but a narrow winding stair to the attic still remains. The original log house kitchen on the grounds, now unused even for storage, is falling apart. A son lives in the house next door; other children and siblings live close by.

I had six brothers and four sisters and helped on the farm just as quick as I got big enough to use a hoe. My father he had us to chop the tobacco, chop the corn, hand tobacco leaves to the loopers, sweep yards, rake yards, anything that had to be done. We started early, about seven o'clock, and if we was filling barns we worked till we finished the barns. If it was a little late, we worked late. And then I helped in the house—iron, wash dishes and do things like that that had to be done.

It wasn't a hard life. We thought it was, but it wasn't. We played when we didn't have nothing to do. I have made playhouses and played different games with first cousins and children that lived nearby. We played prison base, fox-in-the-wall, hide-and-go-seek—all them games back then. Sundays you would go visiting to your aunts and uncles and church.

I was nineteen when I married and have been living here ever since then. I have five children—three live nearby and two about ten miles out. My husband died twenty years ago, but the children were with me. It's been three years that I live alone. Sometimes I mind being alone. But if I can get out with the others where there's different people it's all right. I can come in and lay down and go to bed at night. The worst thing about living alone is that you don't have nobody to speak to unless it's the cat. I have to fuss at him sometimes. That's why I like to get out, you know, and if anyone is doing anything I want to help, 'cause I don't care to be here at the house if I ain't got nothing to do here. I can get out and do something outside. One day I was helping my son in them bushes; then we went and painted a bedroom that evening after we finished. Now in the wintertime . . . I quilted two quilts last winter and finished piecing up one. And then I cook supper for my son, his wife and children at suppertime. They all work and get in late in the wintertime and I fix them supper.

We eat together at night. Oh yes, I eat well. I eat a hearty breakfast and get out and go to work. I worked yesterday evening till near about dark. Mowing this yard. I mow a little bit at a time, that's the way you can keep it down. This big back yard out here goes on back to that cornfield back there and on back to that old feed barn out there. I let that get too big and I ain't got that down. I told them that I wanted to use a Bush Hog [a Bush Hog is a type of mower which is attached to a tractor, and is used on farms to cut down the long grass and tall weeds before cultivating the fields] and cut this down out here 'fore the leaves start falling. Sometimes I feel ordinary common. I don't feel just fine, but I feel good enough to do what I want to do; I am always trying to do something.

No, I don't chew tobacco, I don't smoke, and I don't dip. The only way I use tobacco is to get out here and sheet it up or hand it green or do things like that. I couldn't smoke back when I had too much to do here: my mother-in-law was living and she was sick on the bed, and my husband he had to be waited on too—he had to go on a crutch about nine years. I be so tired at night, I didn't know what to do. I was really tired. I have had to work hard in my days. My husband had arthritis, you know. He had catches all about his hip and his heart was bad and he was too stout. And then my mother-in-law she was down on the bed here for six or seven years. I would see that she got meals, and of course along towards when she got real sick, we had to have somebody here to help out. She stayed right here and I said everything that I done I don't regret nothing I done for her, 'cause they claim they ain't treated too good in a nursing home, they just don't have help enough. I just don't know what can be done. But I know that if there was a patient here that I'd look after them all I could to keep them from having to go. Wouldn't you?

Betty Hunt · 71 · "Running water—If I could get some running water and a bathroom, I'd be the cleanest woman in the county."

Mrs. Hunt, a short, stout, white woman wears her straight graying hair loosely knotted at the nape of her neck. Her smooth skin, fair complexion, and forceful manner belie her age. She is less accepting of life's inequities than many of the other participants.

She lives in a deteriorating house, though her son is making some repairs on it. Progress is very slow and she's pretty upset and unhappy about her house being in such poor condition. She has no running water, no indoor bath, and no telephone.

I'm lonely. But it's not a problem for I don't care about it. I just read and piddle around. Don't do much of anything. I don't go grocery shopping but onc't a month. I wait on Saturday evening and catch my daughter, and she tries to get me to get enough at the grocery to last me awhile.

My daughter's been after me to get me a telephone, but I don't. Cain't afford it. Oh Lord, yeah, if I could afford it, I'd have everything everybody else has got: running water and a bathroom and a telephone. The running water, that's one of the nicest things that anybody could own. I'd rather have it than to have $10,000. That's what I'd love the best. My daughter has got three in her house; one big bathroom and then just, what do they call them, half bath. They're nice. And she works hard for what she's got. I told her when she got as old as I was she wouldn't have sense enough for working too hard to enjoy nothing she's got. The only thing I know is if I could get some running water and a bathroom, I'd be happy. I'd be the cleanest woman in the county, if I had running water. It'd be easy going. It sure would. I just like to get in a kitchen where there's running water. I gets my drinking water from the spring. It's the wonderfulest water, just like it have a piece of ice in it, but it's down in the bottom of the hill and I'm up here.

My daughter, when I'd go visit her, she says, "Mother, you're not going to stand at that sink, I'm going to pack this dishwasher." She packs that. Says, "I'm going wash." She don't do nothing but throw the clothes in the automatic washer and go. Everybody's got convenience but me. Since they got so much stuff piled on the back porch, I cain't pull my old washing machine out. I wash with my hands. Get water out of the rain barrel. I have to hire somebody, anybody I can get, to get me wood, put it in the wood shelter and then I bring it to the porch. If I had a vacuum cleaner, I'd enjoy running it, instead of sweeping with a broom.

If I had one wish, I'd wish my blood pressure would be better and my arthritis wouldn't flare up. If I got sick, to tell you the truth, I don't know what I'd do. I'll just have to leave it up to the family to see what they'd do with me. They'd probably put me in a nursing home. And that's something I wouldn't want. The way I think, the children ought to pitch in and take care of their parents, for they raised 'em and fed 'em and took care of 'em when they couldn't do for theirselves. Well, the young people has so much to do and go. They wouldn't want to be a dragging an old person around, a stumbling, and they wouldn't want to leave me at home by myself. They think a nursing home is just an ideal place for a person.

Everybody in the community thinks that that's the nicest thing that could happen. I don't like it. 'Cause it's too closed in and 'round too many sick people, and I cain't get my freedom to drag out if I wanted to. I do get scared at night a whole lot. My nerves gets bad and I don't sleep, a laying awake waiting for something to happen. There's so much breaking in, and they'll kill you these days for a dollar. So the thought comes across my mind and I get scared, and a cat or a dog will walk up, and that scares me. So, some nights I get up and sit up all night. And when it gets light, I make me a cup of coffee and toast and lay back down and hope I'll doze to sleep, and sometimes I do. But I like to stay here. I don't like a nursing home; I don't care how nice and clean they are. I went to one one time, it was new, they'd just had an open house. And it was so nice and everything and then, oh about two or three months later, some of my friends was there, I went back and it smelt like a wet billy goat. I don't know what made it smell bad to me, and they're just a laying there, tied down—hands tied and tie 'em in a chair—but that's for the benefit of the good of 'em to keep 'em from falling and getting hurt. Tied down in bed, too. 'Cause they didn't want 'em to get up and hurt theirselves climb over the rails of the bed.

I understood it 'cause I had to let my husband stay there 'cause I warn't no nurse and his catheter had to be changed so much and his bladder had to be irrigated so often and I warn't able to have a nurse to stay with him to do it, so there warn't no alternative only to let him stay at the nursing home. I had a little money then and Medicare don't pay after ninety days—you have it then on your own. I paid $577 a month till my money was gone.

He stayed at the nursing home eight months. They don't keep 'em as clean when the mess, you know, the stool gets dried all over, and you'd have to lay wet towels on him to soften it up so you could get it off'n him, lots of times. They sure didn't care for him right, 'cause the doctor had to go in there and use a light on his bottom to try to dry him up. He was galled, just flaming red, and she'd use a light on him, tried to dry him up. So I brought him home the last month. He wanted to come home, and I brought him home and kept him a month till he died and, of course, there was a nurse. I don't know who sent that nurse here. She would come onc't a week and she showed me how to irrigate his bladder, and I did it and it warn't no trouble. If someone had come in before to show me what to do, I would have kept my husband at home. That's what he wanted, and that's what I wanted.

I married just past sixteen years old—I was looking for a better home. I've been living right here in this house for fifty-five years. Lived here and never moved nowhere. We come here the very day we was married. We was married fifty some years—really enjoyed it. He's been dead seven years.

I didn't have a happy childhood. The truth don't hurt nobody. I had to work just like the menfolks did and I didn't think it was right. My daddy thought he was the best man in the world, but he warn't. Our neighbor got sick one spring, he had a big plantation, and daddy told the boys, "Get hitched up. Get hitched up. Get the mules." I was putting water in the washpot to wash, my sister was going clean the yards and work her flowers, and we was going wash windows and curtains and clean up. He come and made us stop and get the hoes and go to work in that field. And that man's seven daughters, nary one of 'em didn't go to the field for nothing. They had a piano and all the notes wouldn't play, and you'd hear every once in a while, bump, bump, bump, bump, and we in their crop at work and that made us real, real angry. I might be ashamed to tell it but I'm not. When he died, I couldn't make a tear come into my eyes.

Was life hard always? Or harder now? Well, now, when people was young and all, they didn't mind nothing they had to do, but old people just cain't do everything. They get disgusted and depressed and any little thing upsets them . . .''

At our final visit to Mrs. Hunt, almost six years later, renovations to the house were nearly complete and indoor plumbing had been installed. We saw a smiling, happy woman. A married granddaughter and her family were living in a trailer on the grounds of her house and a great-granddaughter of four spends most of the day with her, to Mrs. Hunt's obvious delight.

Jane McDonald · 67 · "When I pay all my bills, I don't have much left for groceries."

A short, plump, white woman, Mrs. McDonald is friendly and pleas-ant. She always seems pleased to see us, though her manner conveys a feeling of anxiety.

She lives alone in a deteriorating, frame house of five small rooms. Two of the rooms have a private entrance to accommodate tenants. Mrs. McDonald is afraid to be alone at night, and since her husband's death in 1970, when she has no tenants, she shuttles between her own home and the home of one of her children.

I had a garden last summer and I froze squash, and I canned snap beans, and I canned tomatoes, and these are some of my potatoes. I didn't have too much, but it's really come in good, 'cause groceries are so high. I get food stamps. Oh mercy me, I don't know what I would do without them! The thing about it is this is the first time I have had them in quite a while. When I am not at home I don't get them; I cain't get them when I stay at some of my children's houses.

When I pay all my bills, I don't have much left for groceries. Well, with $109 you don't do much now. When you have the light bill, telephone bill, and the other bills I have, I just don't have much to do with, but they [social services] cain't quite seem to understand that.

Well, I'm thankful for what help I do have, I mean it. Now we have the clinic here, that's the greatest thing we've ever had in Ashton. They get my medicines for me and I don't have to pay for that. The children help me out if I have to get somewhere, but I don't want to have to depend on them all the time. They're real good about helping me if I need something, or maybe sometime they'll bring me some groceries or just a little something. You know, a little something means a lot when you don't have anything. Oh, I couldn't make it without them. I have eight grandchildren and I enjoy them. They always say, "Well Grandma, we love you." And I have real good neighbors and friends. We go to prayer meetings on Wednesday night, then we have services on Sunday morning—that is Sunday school and preaching. Then Sunday night we have our preaching services. I really enjoy that—that is really my life.

A second visit to Mrs. McDonald fifteen months later, in 1977, found her happy to have tenants, a young couple with their infant, to stay in the small apartment. The tenants pay her electric bill as well as their own but pay no rent. Her financial situation, however, had worsened.

According to her report, because of new regulations at the Department of Social Services, she was no longer eligible for the Medicaid assistance [for medications] that she had previously received, nor was she any longer entitled to food stamps. The problem appeared to be that she owned her own home [the condition of which was deteriorating] and owned the ten acres of land on which it stood. The land was not income producing; she grew some vegetables for personal consumption. Nor was she deemed eligible for SSI which we had suggested she apply for.

Mrs. McDonald was struggling with a monthly budget in which everything was paid in installments. Installments on the oil supply, medications [$11 a hundred for heart tablets], the part of her doctor's bill not covered by Medicare, the telephone bill, and lastly, groceries. Her Social Security check—$87 when we first met her in 1973—by this time had reached $111.

A final visit in September 1980 found her back from a period of hospitalization following heat stroke brought on by washing and hanging out clothes, sheets, and blankets, in 97-degree weather. She was living with a daughter.

Georgia Brown · 66 · "I have cooked so much in my days—now I don't cook none at all. I eat sandwiches mostly."

Mrs. Brown, a short, thick-set and heavy-jowled black woman with massive arms is six years younger than her sister, Mrs. Hill, but looks considerably older. Her recently diagnosed diabetic condition possibly accounts for this. She lives in a pink cement block, four-room house on her son's property, within "hollering" distance of his house. Two log cabins, one rented to Mr. Jordan, and two other inhabited, wooden shacks, also sit on this property. Visits in the summer show Mrs. Brown's screen door to be inadequate against flies; in the winter the doors and windows are covered with plastic against the cold. Her small, very warm bedroom is heated with a wood-burning heater (logs are scattered on the floor in a corner of the bedroom); the living room is heated with an oil circulator. A piano in the living room belongs to Mrs. Brown's daughter, as does a large picture of Dr. Martin Luther King, Jr. Grandchildren have attached athletic ribbons to the walls.

When I was born, my mama didn't put it down—my age or nothing. I was born in March. I heard my mama say the first Sunday in March, but I don't even know the year I was born in, but I'm sixty-six I believe.

I been here all my life and my parents lived here all their lives—my mother, my father too. They farmed. They's dead now. Lord, we worked hard. When we was a child and going to school—now this ain't no story—time was so hard, my mama had to wash for some white people up here in Red Hill, and me and my sister [Ola Hill] had to go to the field and pick up corn and carry it to the store and sell it to get flour and meat for us to eat. I had a hard time. I do all the plowing; go to the stable and catch the horses, mules, and plow everyday. I ain't done nothing but a man's work. My sister she stay at the house, but my daddy he'd carry me to the field with him. I'd plow all day long—he'd go off somewhere. When my daddy left mama we had to give up the farm. My mama kept working for white people, washing and ironing, and I just stay 'round the house with my sister and go to school when we could. I didn't get further than the second grade, that's the truth.

I was fifteen when I married and it was better then. My husband farmed till he got disabled—he had diabetes. I sucker tobacco, top tobacco, prime tobacco, and all such as that. He done the plowing. He was sick—I cain't tell you how long he was sick—he's been dead going on three years. I got eight children living, and two dead. All of them have stay right here in hollering distance 'cept one, my oldest [daughter] stay in Washington. Another boy he stay in Raleigh, but the oldest boy of mine stay right over there, right over behind those bushes there. I got a baby son right over that way in a trailer. A daughter stay right there over the hill. All the grandchildren, too, and great grandchildren, sometimes it runs me from home—just too much company. They are here every day, 'cause I look after the grandchildren till my children come home from work. It's, "Grandma gimme this," and, "Grandma gimme that." I said I wish my name was something else 'sides grandma. But like everybody says, I would miss them if they warn't here. And if I couldn't look after myself, some of these children would see after me.

Well, life now it's all right. I stay 'round the house, go to church and Sunday school, and somedays I just go 'round and visit the sick. I got a whole lot o' old people, Miss Eva's brother and Miss Estelle Smith down here, and another lady down the road. I goes 'round and see them, and ask them do they want me to do anything. And most of them want me to do something like help them wash.

I am doing pretty good I should think. The bath is outdoors and the toilet is outdoors, but it don't worry me. I've been used to it all my life. I got hot water and a gas stove, and I don't want nothing no more easier than I got inside the house. I'm just satisfied.

I never did fool with food stamps. I tell you why. Heap o' times they [Department of Social Services] call for you to come down to they place and my children, they at work and all, I never did bother. And I cain't read too good no way. Sometimes, they send me letters I cain't read, so I said well, ain't nobody but me, so I just wouldn't fool with them food stamps. I eat sandwiches mostly—bologna, hot dogs, pimento cheese. I have cooked so much in my days when my husband was living; he wouldn't never eat nothing cold. So now I don't cook unless I have company; now I don't cook none at all. I eat sandwiches mostly. I ain't cooked me no bread since my husband's been dead; I eat loaf bread from the store. I have cooked my part.

I have this diabetes and I goes to the clinic here—they furnish me medicine. They say if all of them would do like I do, they'd get along fine. But since you come the last time I been kinda sick. I cain't do much walking on my legs.

Hattie Bass · 65 · "Ain't nobody in the world can budget with no hundred and some dollars, as high as everything is."

Miss Bass lives in a two-story, eight-room house. Originally painted green, the boards are now weathered and peeling. Although she has given up dairy farming, her nephew continues to keep a few cows on the property and he owns a tractor. Pieces of farming equipment litter the mud-caked yard. We always sat in the kitchen, its bare floor partially covered with torn linoleum, from where we glimpsed a living room meagerly and shabbily furnished.

Miss Bass's tall, thin frame is drably clothed. Her worn, black face is marred by missing and carious teeth.

I was born out there at the water shed when an old house was out there, and that's all the far that I have moved: from there to here. We farmed. All I've ever known all my life is farming. Soon as you got big enough to tote a hoe you went to the field. Then after my mother and father died I still farmed on. Me and my nephew farmed, dairy farming. It just got so we had to hire so much help we just didn't come out. So I stopped farming about five or six years ago.

I been had a hard time all my life. You see, when I was sixteen years old I had T. B. of the bone and had to be under the doctor then for six months. My meal was just a quart of sweet milk a day, and I fell off and didn't weigh anything but ninety-eight pounds. And back then there wasn't no cars like there is now and I had to catch a way, any way I could, to get back and forth to the doctor. I went to Dr. M who stayed down in the bank on the second floor. And he turned the lights on them and healed them up, running sores, and I never broke out no more.

We worked hard. There was eight of us girls and we picked berries. You know they had mules then. While the mules was eating, we'd go out and pick berries and then we'd take them to the store and sell them to get a little money. Carry eggs; we always raised chickens. Mama always had a cow and we had plenty milk and butter, and sometimes she'd take some and carry it to town to get a little money. I believe butter was about thirty cents a pound then. And Sundays we had to go to Sunday school; if you had on shoes, or if you was barefooted, you went to Sunday school and church.

I live on my pension now; Social Security and the gold check, $150. I don't manage, I just have to make out. I told them sometimes I don't even have money left after I pay my bills to buy soap and washing powder to wash my clothes. I get food stamps, but I have to pay $14.00 for those. I used to have to pay $38, they cut it down now to $14.00, and I owed on the house so I had to give it up. It belongs to my nephew, he had to take it over to pay the bill off. I owed $9,400 and some dollars and that's all. So I have to pay rent, $75 a month. That has to come out of my check, so you know there is very little left. Then my light bill and telephone bill. I managed mighty badly this winter, because I got a $105 oil bill now. I burnt more than usual on account of it was so cold and I don't know when it's going get paid, or how I'm going pay it, because my check just ain't that much.

I got running cold water in here but I don't have hot water. A bathroom would make it a whole lot easier. My nephew said when he gets the rent and stuff he would put in a bathroom so I can have running water. I'm a couple of months behind with the rent, but him being my nephew he don't rush me and I pay as I can.

I have went around. I have went to Social Security and I have told them, but they say that's the maximum, and I don't understand it, there ain't nobody can live off of $150. I had to borrow some money to pay my last oil bill; I believe it was $260 some. I got a gas bill too. I've got to pay my light bill, and I got to eat.

Welfare give me the [Medicaid] stickers; I can get my medicine with them. Social Services told me they was going send somebody out here to budget. I said, "Well, you just send them on, and if they can budget what I'm getting and pay my bills, you just tell them to do it." I wish they would. She called me back and said, "It won't be no need of sending nobody out there. You don't get enough to budget." I said, "Ain't nobody in the world can budget with no hundred and some dollars, as high as everything is." And I cain't work. I've had three heart attacks and in July I went back to the hospital and had my gall bladder removed.

Now getting to the hospital for my appointments is some trouble. My nephew's wife, Mattie, works out there and she leaves here before day and I have to get up before day and catch her when my appointment is, you know, then wait till she gets off. A way to get to town would help me a whole lot. There a whole lot of people around here, you know, old people that don't drive and it's just bad. I wish I'd learned to drive. I have to catch anybody I can around here that's going. Sometimes I get out of food and I have to wait till I can get somebody to go get some.

I reckon if I got real sick I'd have to go to a home. I wouldn't want to be no burden on nobody. I been always self-sufficient, do my own thing. I just don't like nursing homes, but I told them that I know I'd have to go there but yet and still I don't like it. A lot of times I just don't believe the people is treated right, like I would treat them if I was working there. Because I have feelings for people, you know, sick people. Now there was a cousin that stayed here and he had to go to a home. He had a stroke, and I couldn't lift him, so he went in this home and I went out there as much as I could to visit him. When he got so he couldn't feed hisself they just set his food down there and go off, and if you cain't feed yourself you just cain't eat! I don't think they treat them exactly right out there.

I'm not lonely. I go visiting. I walk up yonder to Jane and Edgar's house and walk back, and I walk up to Shirley's two or three times a day, and I walk all around here. That's what they told me after I left the hospital with those heart attacks; they told me to walk. So I been walking. I walk right much. I go up to Miss Mangum's up there, Miss Chambers. I like my television pretty good; I like my stories. And I buy a paper and things like that to read. I used to take the daily paper till it went up so high I had to quit it. Went up to $4 and something a month. Yesterday evening I read a book about a dog, a boy and his dog hunting. It was so interesting, I got on it and I kept on till I finished it. Yeah, I read right much.

I have joined the Senior Citizens, about three or four months ago. I went to the Fair with them and learned me how to knit. I used to know, but I had done forgotten, and after they started up that, I renewed it. I made me a cap and I'm making a scarf now if I ever get it done. Sometimes we play bingo, and sometimes we sing, and they have birthday parties down there, and then this summer they carried us down to Bulwer Lake, carried a picnic lunch. I enjoy going around to places, and I enjoy fishing.

There's a half bus load of us. It's not that big bus, it's the small bus. It's fifty-five cents; we pay thirty cents for the ride and put a quarter in the box for our lunch. We enjoy it and we all love each other over there, and look like when one ain't there he's missing, you know. The best thing is to be with people your age, you can talk with them, but these young generations you cain't talk with them. They talk this here young stuff and, you know, we're all old-timey. We're too old-timey for them, I tell them. I've been telling my friends about the Center, if they would just go. At first I thought a lot of them just don't want to go because they'll have to pay fifteen cents, but it seems we have old people who don't want to be old. They want to be young. I think that's what it is. They're afraid that people'll think they're old if they go.

social supports

"If I can help people, that's
about all it takes to make me happy."

Helen Fields · 68 · "I ain't got but one child, but High Lord, he got fourteen children and then he got twenty-one grandchildren, and you know I got a happy life to live."

Mrs. Fields, twice widowed, lives in a trailer behind her son's house. We did not see the inside of the trailer, but the outside had not been painted in a very long time, and the windows were broken. Our interview took place in the basement of her son's house amid a collection of clothes, beds, and old furniture. Mrs. Fields, a smiling, plump black woman, dressed in torn shirt and jeans, a scarf around her head, spitting tobacco juice at regular intervals, peeled and cut up apples for stewing throughout the interview.

I live here in this trailer 'cause I like to be alone sometimes. I cain't get lonely down around here, only sometimes when the children go to school. I got one child and I got fourteen grandchildren from thirty-four down to six. I think the oldest one's thirty-four. One of my granddaughters had a baby three weeks ago. Everytime I turn around I got a great grandchild. I got more great grandchildren than I have grandchildren!

But I'd be pitiful if I didn't live close by them children; I couldn't get nowhere, and all other reasons. Everybody ain't going mess with people. Whole lot of people ain't got no cars, and they ain't got no transportation theirself, and then you ain't got none. So, I thought I'd better stick around that son of mine.

I love children. When there ain't no children around it feels like the house is dead, and nothing cain't function right. When I married Mr. Fields, my second husband, I was living up there in the trailer, and one night I told him this is a lonesome house. He say, "Why don't you go down there and get one of them boy-children. He's got enough of 'em to divide." So I took him at his word, and I went down there asking for one of 'em. My son say, "I don't know, mama. Which one you want?" I say I want the little boy, Willie. He say, "I'll have to see about it, see what Mildred [his wife] say." You know, people don't like to part from their children, nohow. Well, one day Willie got hurt, got his hand caught in the washing machine, and my son decided it was 'cause there's so many of 'em there and they play so rough. So he bring him to me. He was four years old. Bad little boy. Mischievous. Always into something. I raised him from four years old on up till now. He's grown and gone now.

Every night one of the little boys stay with me. I don't like to stay up there in the trailer too much by myself, not at night. I look at T.V. a whole lot, and you see what's going on you get kind of nervous. You know, people done got so they're terrible.

The worst thing now is these children; they uses so much dope in school. I be worried to death 'bout these little boys around here. Like when they get out at night, you don't know what's going happen, whether they're going come in or whether somebody's going call. That's why I don't want a telephone. Telephone wake me up way in the night, it'd scare me to death. I just don't want to get involved with no polices.

Now we ain't had so much trouble with drinking around here. None of my grandchildren are drinking but one. That one I raised, I never seen him high but one time. He had drunk some home-brew, he say, and it made him sick. Some children brought him home. I looked at him and commenced praying. I say, "Lord, I ain't got to go through with this, is I?" I say to Willie, "I'll talk to you when you get all right." The drink made him so sick and I was so glad. Next day he say, "Lord ha' mercy, I'll never do that no more." And I ain't seen him had no more drink.

But young folks don't have time to fool with old folks. A whole lot of people don't like to mess with old folks. Take for instance they have these young folks waiting on old folks in nursing homes and they ain't good to 'em, not at all. Some young folks treat 'em terrible, like dynamite. I'm useful now. I helps Mildred with the cooking and the cleaning, I mend the boys' clothes and I make quilts. And I been working with the tobacco crop—we started barning tobacco yesterday —but sometimes I feel like I ain't doing, cain't do my duty. Cain't get up and do like I have done, I reckon, but I've been use to working all my days, ever since I've been big enough and can remember.

The best time of my life was when I was growing up and when I was working at the factory. 'Cause you keep your mind busy and don't have nothing to worry 'bout but your job.

Now, when I feels sick, Lord, it's been a big help having that clinic here. I told them that's the best thing that happen in this community. I don't know what we'd do without it. If anytime, anything, if you feel bad and something happen, you get on the phone, call down there, somebody's going come and get you.

I gets some Social Security. It ain't enough to live on, but I try to make out the best I can. I ain't went and tried for food stamps—tell you the truth, my brains ain't functioning right to start it—I don't know how to do it. I didn't go to school much, just till the second grade.

I cain't grumble. Life's been pretty good with me; I don't think I want to change it, not now. I am happy with it just like it is. I don't be always complaining, I don't be sick all the time, and I can get up every morning by the help of the good Lord and I can say, "Thank you, Jesus, I've got another bright day in the front of me." I go to church and I have a happy life. I ain't got but one child, but High Lord, I got one child and he got fourteen children and then he got twenty-one grandchildren, and you know I got a happy life to live. I look at my son sometimes and I say, "Lord ha' mercy. If I had had two or three children and they had as many children as you got, I would've been head over heels with children wouldn't I?" I'm happy just like I am. All I need is a porch to my trailer, and I think I'd be real happy. Sit out there in the mud and the sun.

Alma Wright · 75 · "My children all say I am not going into a rest home; as long as they got a home I can rest in their homes."

Mrs. Wright, a good-looking, white woman, is under five feet in height. Her posture, skin, and muscle tone betray her age, but her vigor, vitality, and mental alertness are those of a far younger woman. Dressed in shorts she still mows her lawn and works her garden.

Mrs. Wright lives in a five-room, brick ranch house built in the fifties. An enclosed porch off the kitchen is used for putting up her garden produce. Many family photographs adorn the walls of her house. Particularly arresting ones are those of Mrs. Wright herself as an attractive young woman and a strikingly beautiful photograph of her mother.

My husband died twelve years ago. We had a big farm. I stayed on right here and attended my garden. My son does the plowing. My son-in-law has a tractor. Whichever one goes out when it needs plowing, plows my garden. Two of my children live next door to me. I used to go over there at night or they would come over here. I just rather stay at home, though. It was a right smart trouble just to go. We had an intercom—if I went to sleep first they could hear me snoring! If my son or daughter want to go somewhere the same weekend, I either go to my daughter in Winston-Salem or else I go with one of them.

When I need groceries, I either go with my daughter or my son or give them my grocery list and they bring it to me. I usually keep plenty on hand in case something happens—I even keep my bread froze. But my freezer's so full now I don't have room for no bread because I had my garden, and I canned seventy quarts of snap beans and I don't know how many quarts of butter beans and squash. I canned some apples and some tomatoes and green beans. I got more stuff here than I can eat in a year's time. I say every year that I am not going to have a garden next year, but when the time come I can't wait to get out there.

I worked as a child. Of course we was raised to work and I loved to work. I raised my children to work. I learned from experience if you teach a child to love to work when he's little, when he grows up he will love to work. I think the most pitiful thing in the world is a lazy grown person that won't work. A lazy teenager that won't work will go out there and join the club and carry on. Like Patricia Hearst—she didn't have to work, her parents were rich.

I walked three miles to school and the road was so red, muddy. We use to leave home 'fore light and get home the stars was shining. We wore union suits, and you pulled your stockings up and fastened them with supporters and wore high-top shoes. My stepmother had an education and I got education at home. I couldn't concentrate at school really; where we went there was seven grades in one room and one teacher.

I have a son-in-law that can do anything. When I had to get a new commode he put that in, and I got a new sink in my bathroom and he installed that for me, and this water is bad about eating up spigots so he has put on three of those for me. If anything goes wrong with my well pump, he fixes that and he won't take no pay. My children buy my clothes and bring them to me. But I'd like one more time to go to the store and fit them on myself.

I have plenty to do. I play the piano or I watch T.V. or I can play solitaire. I do some reading—the Bible is 'bout the only thing I care 'bout reading. I do my own sewing, and I used to do a lot of crocheting. I made quilts and I made bed spreads. I still play baseball with the grandchildren; I can still knock a ball a long way! I go to church when I feel like it; sometimes, though, I have this dizziness. When I'm sick like that one of my children will get off and carry me to the doctor, and the doctor said the dizziness comes from inner ear trouble and I have to keep pills on hand to take for that dizziness. I've been in the church all my life—I was raised right next door to the church.

My children all say I am not going into a rest home; as long as they got a home I can rest in their homes. So I just hope and pray God's will won't be I have to stay in a rest home. I suppose high-rise housing for the elderly in town is all right unless a fire breaks out or something like that. I don't think they are safe because I have seen them on T.V. where some would be jumping out of the windows, and it was a lot that got burned up and all those things. I would rather stay in my own house and have somebody come in and kind of do what had to be done. There's one thing I want to know. If you really have to go into a rest home would you have to go ahead and start off signing over everything you got to them before you can go? It was so one time that people that had something they would take a lien on it, and people that didn't have anything went scot-free. I don't think that's fair. 'Cause the children helped work and accumulate what you have, and all that work is wasted. And some people wouldn't work in a pie factory and never has tried to accumulate anything, they fare better. [Working in a pie factory is considered a desirable job because the work is light and employees can eat as many pies as they like. A person who wouldn't work in a pie factory is, therefore, a very lazy person.] They can go free and get all the attention they need and don't have to pay anything. I don't think that's fair.

Emma Mitchell · 91 · "Unless I visit my children, I don't miss one Sunday going to church. I am the oldest one."

On our first visit to Mrs. Mitchell, she had a lady living with her who did most of the housework, but, according to her daughter, "this lady was in her eighties, and two ladies together. . . . She tried to tell mother how to do her own home and mother didn't like that, you know."

Of medium height and slight build, her small, pointed, pale face crowned with abundant silky white hair, Mrs. Mitchell is remarkably spry for her ninety-one years. Married for fifty-eight of those years, she was seventy-eight when her husband died. Since his death—because she lives in close proximity to two of her children and has very frequent visits to and from her other five children and her sister in Ashton—she has not spent a night alone in her house.

Her gracious, two-story house is situated in a grove of oak trees. It is spacious, well appointed, and contains all the amenities necessary to ensure comfortable living. In good health, and obviously pleased and proud of her longevity and independence, Mrs. Mitcbell has a happy, active, and friendly personality.

My father was a farmer and I had ten brothers and sisters. I was the third child, so when I finished school I stayed home with mother to help look after a baby or help her keep house. We had a colored woman come to rub our laundry on a board—we didn't have electricity then out here. I was twenty when I married and I just stayed at home and we visited. I always went to Sunday school and church. We didn't have too much of anything, but we would have a few parties and it was a good life. I had a good husband as anybody could have, I think. He was a railroad man, engine operator. We were married fifty-eight years. He died when he was eighty-two—the twenty-fifth of this month he will have been dead thirteen years.

Well, after my husband died, I stayed close to my children and they would come visit. When he died all my children were married. My son lives right down here, I have a daughter in Mill Town, and then I have my oldest daughter in Greenville, South Carolina, a son in Kentucky, ones in different places, you know. Seven altogether. I see my son every day. I don't see my daughter every day because sometimes she sews, and she's a widow too. We could've lived together, but I wanted to stay at home and she wanted to stay at home. I have stayed with my children a whole lot down in South Carolina, but I'm happier when I'm in my own house. Even when I'm with my children—and they have been as good to me as anybody could be—I'd rather stay home than anywhere else, if I can get someone to stay with me. I have a lady that comes in, and she does most of the work with my help. She hasn't been here too long. And I never stay here alone at night. My children will call me and come around, and I go there. I don't have to have nobody do much for me, just once in a while. I don't have to depend on anybody |for money|. My son looks after everything for me, the farm with about one hundred sixty acres of land, and the house on the corner of the road over yonder that I rent to Mrs. Ward.

If I live to April, I'll be ninety-one years old. Twenty years ago I had this breast removed, and then about a year ago I had the other one partly removed—it was malignant but not as bad as this one. I haven't been well recently, though; I went to Mill Town Hospital and stayed a week. I was just so dizzy and my head was hurting me terrible. The doctor wanted me to come over and take x-rays. He said I was doing pretty good—I have angina but not too bad. When I came back home I was sick again so my son and his wife stayed here two weeks on their vacation. While they were here, once in a while I'd have a hard chill, and they would put hot pads on my arm.

I can see real well for my age, and I love to read. I like to read the day's paper, my church books. I go to church every Sunday. I didn't go last Sunday because I had been sick, but I'm planning to go this Sunday. Unless I visit my children, I don't miss one Sunday going to church. I'm the oldest one in my church and my sister, Charlotte Walker, is the next oldest.

Charlotte Walker · 86 · "I go to church every Sunday that comes; I never miss a Sunday from Sunday school and church."

Mrs. Walker lives in a spacious, two-story house, immaculately kept, solidly furnished and set among large trees on about an acre of land. The household contains all amenities, including a washer and dryer. The attractive, wide front porch is decoratively inset with red tiles. An old "potato house," which looks like a child's log cabin playhouse is no longer in use for storing vegetables, but is a reminder of times gone by. Except for her tunnel vision (after removal of cataracts five years ago), and increasing deafness, she manages extremely well and still does all her own housework, laundry and cooking.

A pleasant, friendly woman with short gray hair and a lightly freckled face, Mrs. Walker is mentally alert, physically fit, very sociable, and interested in community affairs.

Five years is how long I've been living alone. Daytime, not at night. The lady across the road, my sister-in-law, [Betty Hunt] stays with me at night. I have never stayed in this house a single night by myself—I cain't lie down in this house and go to bed by myself—I never have. My sister-in-law doesn't like to stay by herself either. She comes over most of the time after supper. We don't get up until about eight o'clock in the morning and she eats breakfast with me. My nephew and his wife come here every Friday night after supper, and they stay here until supper on Sunday night, and then go back to Wilson.

Twice a month I get together with the ladies. Wednesday we will have the Home Demonstration Meeting. Somebody carries me there when I go. We have a luncheon meeting and we enjoy it a lot. A lot of ladies don't come because they really don't get out as much as they should. When they do get out you will hear them say, "Well, I really didn't have time to come today." They don't hear me say that, because I don't do anything much. We are working on getting a fellowship hall now as hard as we can; we have about $14,000 now. I don't often get to the club's council meeting anymore—it meets once a month. The club has one big meal a year for senior citizens. I would go to the Senior Center if I didn't have to be so careful about my eyes. (I had an operation for cataracts five years ago). I'm afraid I stay at home too close on account of that. But I go to church every Sunday that comes; I never miss a Sunday from Sunday school and church.

Now I don't know whether one of these programs with meals for the elderly would work out here. I think it's right nice in Mill Town where so many of those elderly people live in those housing units. But out in the country they are so scattered, I don't know how successful you would be at that. Most of us, if we cain't do it ourselves, we have somebody in to help us.

I try to cook a little of everything that I should. I had brunswick stew for dinner; I bought a quart from the Ruritans. They have a brunswick stew and barbecue once a year; they are very active. They have never quite finished paying for the building because if you all have noticed, the Ruritan building is a nice building and it costs a lot, as much free labor as it had on it (we have a brick mason that builded the fireplace for nothing). Under the fireplace on a plaque it says this land is donated in memory of my husband. I didn't ask them to do it. I didn't even know they were doing it until one of the boys came over here one night and asked me to come over to the Ruritan hut. I gave them four acres of land.

I've been getting along all right, except I am not happy with my eyes, but I just got to live with that. So I don't worry about that too much. In June, I reckon it was the first of June, I had a hysterectomy. And Dr. —— said that it was the most amazing thing he'd ever seen. You know I had the cancer smear and it showed up abnormal a little. And he said if I would go ahead and have the hysterectomy that everything would be behind me, then I wouldn't have a thing in the world to worry about. And he said that I was in the best condition of a woman my age (I will be eighty-six Friday). Well, I felt a little weak and bad when I came home, but I was up walking the next day after I had the operation. My niece stayed with me and my sister-in-law stayed sometimes.

Did you know that I had an older sister? Emma Mitchell is my sister. She's ninety years old and lives in a house sort of like this one up on in the oak grove. Now our mother and father, neither one didn't live long.

My daddy wasn't but seventy-five and my mother wasn't but seventy-six. And when my mother died I thought she was a real dead old woman, but if I could see real good I wouldn't think about my own self being old!

Isaac Long · 71 · "An old man just need somebody with him in the house."

Mr. Long smiles broadly, his large, widely spaced teeth showing white in his dark black face. He is over six feet tall and well built, his face is unwrinkled; his hair and moustache are beginning to gray.

Mr. Long owns his compact, four-room white house which is situated on a narrow dirt road. A patch of garden faces the railroad tracks. The house is heated by an oil circulator in the living room. A small but full bathroom, an electric kitchen stove, and an old refrigerator provide modestly adequate amenities. Besides family photographs, two good-sized reproductions of landscapes hang on the living room wall. The upholstered sofa and love seat are comfortable but worn.

I done all kinds of work when I was grown. Sharecropping, cleaning dairies, looking after beef cattle. I work at Mill Town Hospital, I be a janitor, for ten years 'fore I retired. I still works when there's some to do. I tends Mr. C's place; I keeps his family graveyard mowed off, and I tends a big garden for him.

Sure I had fun when I was growing up. I start to work when I was big 'nough—'bout five or six. Did everything that needed it. It was better times then, but now, children get more different things to see and different things to go to in the community than they did then. We just worked and played. Now a child got to go to school dressed up, eat the very best of food—we eat what we could. Soul food. Strong stuff. Molasses and butter, eggs and chicken and all such as that. We raise our own chickens and make our molasses. Old folks raise everything they eat.

I went to school right down here in Red Hill till 'bout the seventh grade. You had to learn a book then, it ain't like it is now. Them books were hard. You had to stay in there two years till you learned it. Now they pass you every year.

I'll be dog if I know what was the best time of my life; I had a good time all the time. I don't let nothing worry me. But I suppose now is the best time. I gets Social Security and the hospital pays a little pension as well, $15 a month; I don't get any other help at all. I wouldn't mind something to help me out to get my medicine. I declare it's tight now! My high blood medicine cost me more than $10 a month. But I'm making out. I takes care of myself now better and I goes to church, Sunday school, I sings in the men's chorus, and I don't run 'round nowhere at all, and I don't drink whiskey and I don't smoke.

I quit drinking whiskey 'bout thirty years; I've been quit smoking 'bout ten years. I ask the Lord to help me, take the taste away from me. It left me too, right then. I told Him I'd never drink no more whiskey. Drink—I was high every Saturday and Sunday, Christmas time, like that. I wouldn't raise no sand. I just laughed and had fun, but the foolishness of a man, a person that drinks, drinks, drinks. I just got tired of it.

Use to be moonshine 'round, maybe some 'round here now I reckon, somewhat. But Lord, it use to be you could get a drink of whiskey as quick as you could get a drink of water, and the law stood in with the bootleggers. That's the truth. I use to know all the people who make it, but nobody don't tell nothing 'round here. They shoot 'em. Anybody tell anything out here, your house'll get burned up, they'd kill 'em. Like that man that live right over there, Burton, right 'cross the railroad there in a mansion, somebody kill him and his wife both and burn 'em up. I declare the world's something! You just got to tend to your business, that's all you can do. I don't know what's the matter with folks. Just goes crazy and they shoot.

I was married before when I was younger; we separated and got a divorce. This here lady, the second one I married, she died two years ago going on three years. Now I cooks for myself, cleans my house, do my own washing and everything. The worst is I just ain't got nobody with me. Ain't but one thing I need. An old man just need somebody with him in the house.

When I was sick back here in last February, I didn't even come out to outdoors till they carry me to the doctor. I stay in the house. Weak, if I try to get up like to answer the telephone, I just be liable to fall or sit down. See, when you stay by yourself you just need somebody, a person in the house, 'cause you don't know what's going to happen. Course everybody's got to die, but sometime you save a person by just somebody being there that could do something for 'em. You know, I might get so sick I cain't get to the telephone. So I'm going marry a lady I got acquainted with in Capital City. She's 'bout the age my wife was, a pretty little woman. She's a Christian-hearted woman, a good woman.

I think me and her will make it. She's a little younger than I am, not much.

I wouldn't have a young woman. A young woman, good gracious alive, they'll worry you to death. She'd want everything you making and Lord, Lord, all your money! Now I have heard tell of a man, 'bout my age I reckon, that just got crazy 'bout a girl, old as he was, a good-looking, nice-looking girl. She draw his check and everything, then she made him will her his house and everything he had to her. Old man got old and she took and put him in a home, sold that place and left.

During a visit to Mr. Long a year after the first interview, we met his new wife. The marriage was a success. As Mrs. Long reported, "My daughter and I lived together. She had a bunch of grown girls so she had a plenty of company when I was away. So I thought I'd come down here and see how I like it, and I liked it fine. It ain't hard for me to live with Isaac; he's good to get along with. Yeah, we two old people was lonely. He didn't have anybody and I didn't either. We got together. Now he's happy like a jaybird."

Julia Lewis · 83 · "I feel like children are responsible for their parents, that it's their place to look after them instead of expecting the community to."

Mrs. Lewis was left partially paralyzed following a stroke in 1973. Still mentally alert, she is unable to walk and is without the use of her left arm and hand. Mrs. Lewis is dependent on the care of a dutiful daughter-in-law and son who accept their roles as the natural obligation of children.

We conducted the following interview with the daughter-in-law during her lunch break in the Ashton Post Office in which she works part-time.

I think the reason why some can stay home and some can't goes back to the original make-up of the person. Part of this is your individual characteristics, like willingness to work and a determination to have things of your own like you want. Mom Lewis wanted her own things and she knew how she wanted them kept, and she worked to have them that way. All of her life she worked hard, and she and Pop saved for a rainy day thinking that this type thing might happen. They pinched pennies so that if it came they could do it this way. Really, that's why she's where she is now, and why she's able to do it without being a burden to taxpayers or to someone else. She's doing it with her own means. They worked hard and saved all their lives, and of course they worked more than eight hours a day, as most farmers do. Their desire had been to wear out instead of rust out. They had said this over the years. Pop Lewis operated a sawmill until World War II, then he went into poultry farming. Both of them grew up on farms before they was married. They was later than usual marrying—he was thirty-eight and she was twenty-seven. There was ten years difference in their ages, but they celebrated their fiftieth anniversary just three or four months before he died.

Mom Lewis had the stroke in April of '73. She was two months in the hospital and two months in the nursing home, and then we brought her home in September with hired help. There's always someone with her twenty-four hours. She needs complete care. She can feed herself, but everything else has to be done including keeping the house and caring for her. We have everything that we need to care for her. We have a wheel-chair, so we can get her up every day and take her outside. I do that, because it's a little harder out-of-doors on the person pushing her and on her too. She reads some but not too much. Bob carried her last week for an eye check-up because she said, "I can't see." The doctor adjusted her glasses, but it had been less than a year since we had had the glasses changed, so there's nothing more that can be done. The left hand is useless, but the right hand is good. The therapist was working on this for a while, and we were hoping she would get so that she could crochet again because this would pass the time. She used to like to crochet. She watches T.V. which I think she enjoys; it is a blessing to shut-ins. I wouldn't say she eats well. She eats breakfast good. We have balanced meals for her, but she does not eat well at the other two meals. And of course she gets vitamins. She does sleep well. We are blessed in that she has a good night. We put her to bed and seldom have to get up with her during the night.

It hasn't been easy to get a helper. This is helper number nine in two years! We've had all different kinds. It's hard to find a good one and keep her. Nobody we get is a professional nurse except the public health nurse who comes and changes the catheter. They will come on call anytime we ask them to and of course the county pays for that. And we did have a physical therapist for a while, but she got busy and anyway there is no hope for fundamental improvement.

When one helper gives out we run ads, we ask people to pass the word around that we are looking, we contact the health services, the public-health workers. The job is fully explained, the responsibilities, pay and the time off, before they accept the job. The woman who helps us now works twelve days on and two days off, and this is what she agreed to before she came here. I relieve every other weekend. I have one elderly colored woman [Lola Buchanan] who is seventy-five that works on the Saturday morning of the weekend that I relieve. Long enough for me to do my four hours here at work. The young lady that is helping us now is thirty years old and we have a twenty-six-year-old colored woman. Both of them have had mental problems of their own, but they were not so severe that they could not do this type work and we were willing to take people who had mental breakdowns in the past. They both had had other jobs, but there are a lot of people that would hold that against them and wouldn't even give them a chance.

The neighbors have been very gracious about calling on her. Of course, she's been active in the church and the community. Some of the neighbors are older people, her age, but we also have our friends that call on her. Some of the young people that call on her do it out of their regard for her and not for us.

So far as what we do, there again, it is individual make-up. I feel like children are responsible for their parents and that it's their place to look after them instead of expecting the community to. So really, that is the story as far as I am concerned. I grew up with it. My mother looked after her mother-in-law when I was twenty. My father had been the youngest son and he inherited the homeplace with provision that she lived there, but we were taught to respect and do for Granny the things that she needed to have done. So it has been ingrained I suppose. It takes sacrifice, but it takes sacrifice unless you stick them in a nursing home and never go to see them. It takes sacrifice to go and see them daily, and with the condition she was in when she was in the nursing home, you could not be satisfied without going daily. So there is no easy out.

One reason we try to keep her at home is that we think she is happier here than she would be anywhere else. Now don't pin too many stars on me, because if it came to giving up my part-time work, instead of putting her in a nursing home, I might give in and put her into a nursing home. There is probably not a lot of years left for Mom and in this particular job if I gave it up they would have to get somebody else and it would be gone. I enjoy my work as well as saving for that rainy day that may come to my life.

I think nursing homes are good and they serve a purpose, but there is much to be desired. We had four months' experience with one, and some of the people working there are doing all they can. Of course, they got some sorry help too. They are limited in the caliber of help that they get. Some of them are just as kind as can be and do more than eight hours' work in their eight hours there. Others you see in the hospitals as well as the nursing homes, hide behind the corners and have their little friendly visits with somebody else down the hall. But if I were attending to ten people, I couldn't do everything needed either, so there is always something to be desired.

I suppose if you total up everything, it's almost as expensive to keep a person at home by the time you count the maintenance of the house, even though it's their own home, and fees for the helpers. Of course, we have had different fees. We have not paid everybody the same because they set their own fee. One of them was even $110 a week, but we have gotten by, usually with not paying more than $80 a week. The only thing Medicare does is pay for the therapist's visits. I would assume that the public health nurse costs would come from the county.

I don't think we are remarkable, and I don't think we deserve any praise, really. People used to look after their parents all the time. I feel that now a lot of people are not doing what they should be doing. As I said, I feel like it's a child's obligation. But it takes responsibility, and I don't know that you can legislate the things that will make it work because it's a personal characteristic in each case.

When we visited old Mrs. Lewis in her own house, we found her sitting in a kind of day chair, leaning back watching T.V. She was very pleased to see us, and we spoke to her for about ten or fifteen minutes. Her usual day passes very slowly and she was happy to have our company.

Mrs. Lewis spoke to us of her past; of her husband to whom she had been married for fifty years and with whom she had been very happy. She also spoke of the beauty of the outdoors and how near to tears she had been that morning knowing that she would have to remain indoors until her daughter-in-law returned home from work. She sang her daughter-in-law's praises, telling us what a marvelous daughter-in-law she has. She is moved by the attentions of people who visit her, particularly the Sunday school class she has taught.

Within the short time of our visit, Mrs. Lewis expressed an array of emotions. She wept several times as she spoke of the frustrations presented by her disability and total dependence on others. And there were moments of pride and joy as she told us about her happy marriage and her satifaction in having lived so long.

Mary Collins · 85 · "She don't have any friends that come around. She always tried to go sit with somebody else; when it come a time for somebody to come sit with her, she don't have anyone."

Mrs. Collins, a tall, slender, neatly dressed, black woman, apparently suffers from a form of familial deafness. Her daughter reports that her mother and her mother's three sisters have all been deaf ever since she can remember.

Mrs. Collins lives next door to her daughter in a four-room, deteriorating house with no indoor plumbing. She still keeps this house but, at her daughter's request, has recently moved into her daughter's home. Her daughter is a chore worker for the County Department of Social Services and is away during the day, so Mrs. Collins is usually alone until the grandchildren come home from school.

Mrs. Collins is not eligible for a chore worker herself, because she is ambulatory, can cook for herself, and can tend to her own personal hygiene. County funds for chore workers are limited, workers are hard to find in rural areas because transportation costs are not reimbursed, there is a two- to three-month waiting list, and clients are served on a priority basis.

Since it was not possible for us to communicate with Mrs. Collins directly, the interview was conducted with her daughter.

I've been with my mother all my life; I haven't moved away. She can read my lips pretty well, and I do a lot of actions and motions. She is not too well just now—she's just out of the hospital. She had a major operation, female trouble, at age eighty-five. But the doctors are pleased with her progress.

She came over to my house two years ago. Course her house, which is next door, is still furnished with her furniture. We thought it wasn't too safe for her to stay alone since she cain't hear too well. And it's better on me by being in my house, so I can cook for her, do her washing and what-not same time I do mine. So it just makes it better on both of us.

We don't have running water or a bathroom at this time. We're working at it very hard and hope in the near future . . . maybe at the end of the year we will be in the process of building a home behind this one. But she manages very well. She hasn't been bedridden so far, but it would be a problem if she couldn't get outside.

Before this spell of sickness, she could stay here alone in the day-time. She was very active. I work, but it so happen I planned to be home for two weeks on vacation right now. I'm hoping after two weeks she may be able to stay all alone during the day. I have a sister and a brother that live in Mill Town, and if she cain't stay alone after two weeks, we will have to make some other arrangements.

Day care for elderly? It would be helpful to me, but it kind of makes it hard with her to communicate with other people—that would be the only thing. For instance, if she had a ride to go somewhere every day it'd be kind of hard 'cause she'd feel kind of . . . I don't know . . . left out 'cause she cain't hear what you are saying. I think she'd like it though, if it became a habit. I mean she might get used to it after making friends with someone else. She's lonely now. She don't have any friends that come around. She always tried to go sit with somebody else; when it come a time for somebody to come and sit with her, she don't have anyone. Most of her friends I'd say are sick themselves. The people from the Missionary Circle come and visit. They don't have no set time, different members just come in and out, come in and out, at their convenience I'd say. I have three children. I think she can understand a child better than she can an adult. Old people seems to be a little childish anyway.

She's not getting food stamps, but she'd like to. I took her down to Social Service about a year ago and she wasn't eligible at that time. See, it's another thing—she's living with me. It's hard to get many services when she's not living alone. I'm a social worker, but we're classified as homemakers, and I work with different people—mostly elderly. We help them with money management, housing, we transport them back and forth to the hospital, medical centers and what-not. It's a pretty big job. I don't think she [my mother] would be eligible for an attendant—the guidelines are pretty strict. Only if she lived in her own home she might would be eligible for this service.

Lillian Adams · 71 · "If I can know that I can see people, and I can help people, that's about all it takes to make me happy."

Miss Adams lives in a pleasant, almost circular cluster of five or six houses, tucked behind a country store and placed at the end of a narrow lane. Her family home, white and freshly painted, has eight comfortably furnished rooms. We noted an antique pie chest in her kitchen. Bright, flowering plants in big containers decorate the front porch as does an old-time double swing, suspended from the rafters.

Her light brown hair is brushed straight back from a high forehead; her face is intelligent and alert. Miss Adams, always on the move, is a natural helper in the community where she is highly respected. After teaching school for forty-four years, she has been retired for the past five years and busies herself with church and other volunteer activities. Never married, she is close to her brothers and sister whom she sees frequently and has many friends throughout the community. Still driving a car, she uses it to get to and from her volunteer organizations, to visit elderly shut-ins, to transport needy friends to town for food stamps, or for other important errands.

My parents farmed. I helped by dropping tobacco plants, from about eight or nine years old on. We had to plant with a peg; we dropped plants. One thing I didn't like to do and never did do is to hoe. That was always too tedious for me. And then, when we started housing the tobacco, we were always there to hand up the leaves and things like that. I don't know which was better, the old days or now. I haven't farmed any in the "now" way.

I finished school here, then went to college nearby. I didn't know what I was going to do when I went. I really wanted to go into the medical field, but then I just started teaching. I stayed here with my mother and daddy and taught up here at the elementary school. After my daddy died, I was here with my mother and then I went on to the high school here to teach. When my mother died in '68, this place was left to the children. So, my three brothers and sister just signed their part over to me, and, naturally, they come to visit and call it home.

I take it day-by-day. That's what makes me happy, I guess. I know you've got to plan ahead, but if I stopped to think what I'm going to be doing five years from now and start concentrating on that, then I'll forget what I'm supposed to do today. Of course, now, you know yourself that times come in your life when you have to meet a crisis and things of that kind, but we've always been able to meet them some way or other. Even during the depression, my brother said, "I know that 1932 was a real warm winter. The grass in the yard stayed green just like it is out here, the whole winter long." My brother said, "Well, I know the Lord knows what He's doing in this weather business because there are many people don't even have shoes."

It doesn't take so much to make me happy like it does a lot of folk. If I can know that I can see people and people can come to see me, and I have something decent to wear and something to eat, and I can help people, that's about all it takes to make me happy. I do more for people now than I did when I was younger, like cooking things for people, carrying them, sharing vegetables with those who can't help themselves.

Now my mother was in a nursing home four years after she fell off the bed and broke her hip. That nursing home was owned by four doctors, privately owned, and the superintendent was a very efficient R.N.; in fact, she visited every patient every day. We were satisfied with that, but I understand that now at that same nursing home, the doctors have sold out to somebody in New York or Maryland or somewhere like that. I think what we need in nursing homes is a personal interest, not somebody way up yonder somewhere owning it and just employing anybody who will take a job. Of course now, my brothers and sister won't be satisfied to have me go to a nursing home. All of them have said, "Come, live with me." But now, going and doing it is two different things.

I think, maybe, the biggest thing we need here would be a full time doctor. We had a doctor here some years ago. For instance, when my mother had an edema and took real sick at three o'clock in the morning, I didn't know what it was. I just said, "Well, I'll have to go get the doctor, because this is different than anything we've ever had." So, I just ran across the road over there at three o'clock in the morning and the doctor says, "I'll be there in fifteen minutes." And she was here. Ordinarily you have to pick up a person like that and take them to the hospital, or call an ambulance. Now, I have registered at this Community Health Center out here. I haven't had to use it yet, fortunately, but I have heard people who have used it say it's satisfactory. What people really want, though, is a private doctor. They want somebody that they think will come into the home in the middle of the night.

Polly Williams · 75 · "The people here in the community, neighbors, we check on each other."

Miss Williams is a retired school teacher who was born and brought up in the small community in which she now lives . She is small and slightly built; her increasing deafness, stooped shoulders, gnarled hands and wrinkled face are evidence of physical aging. However, her mind is clear and she is forthright in her opinions. (At the time of our original survey she half jokingly called one interviewer a "Yankee carpetbagger," and talked about the havoc wrought on the community by the Civil War.)

Miss Williams lives in a five-room house with indoor plumbing, but, because of her deafness, she has no use for a telephone or television set. Attractive semicircular stone steps lead to a wide porch with rocking chairs and an old-fashioned swing. The house is one of a group situated at the back of a country store, secluded from the traffic but within minutes of the main Ashton highway. A small organ stands against one wall of her narrow living room. She spends a good deal of time cooking and baking in her kitchen, which is the largest room in the house. She also keeps busy visiting sick friends and neighbors, and is active in the concerns of her church and community.

I liked life better in the old days; the freedom and the love and the respect that all people, all races, black and white, had for each other. We didn't make much distinction. And children didn't demand so much then. When we got a little we were happy. Now they get a little bit and they are unhappy.

I'm not lonely. I pass the day doing a little housework, neighbors coming in, and I do a lot of visiting. Some days I walk five miles and some days two, and some days just around the house. I used to love to sew and crochet but I don't see well now. I've given all my quilts away. And I've given away all my dishes and everything of value to my two nephews and my niece. I bake a lot and give away most of what I cook. There are some people in the village who are incapacitated and I help them a lot. But somebody is bringing me something in all the time. One neighbor just came in with a bowl of potato salad and another came in with green peas and corn.

You are a little bit confused about my education—I am really very ignorant. I only had the usual number of years of schooling, high school and college, but our high school education was nothing. To go from the seventh grade to high school I was asked to copy some pages in the back of a grammar book. I didn't know what it meant. "Shall have been" was the verb form that I didn't know at that time—that was all I had to know to go to the high school. I think my education was very poor.

After college I taught school, the first grade, for forty years. I wish I was still at it; I've been retired ten years. Sometimes a great big burly man gets up and gives me a hug and I have to find out who he is. I've taught three generations. I never did teach any blacks because they weren't in the schools at that time. But they lived on the farm—did sharecropping or farmed on halves—and we worked together, helped each other. I had a little red Chevrolet and I lived down about five miles on my daddy's farm when I was teaching. If I couldn't start the car, any trouble, I would go out and ring the dinner bell and they knew exactly what was wrong. One sleety morning I tapped it and here they came, jumped in the car with me, started it, and with their axes cut the trees out of the road all the way up to the main road. No thanks and no pay—no nothing. If I was going to town, and they needed a ride, they rode in with me. That is the life we lived and that is the life I like.

Today we lack competent teachers as well as competent people in all walks of life because things have been so easy for them. They don't put forth much effort. Seems like there is a little flaw in their upbringing, a character failure. People don't discipline themselves enough, young and old. The trouble is they don't believe in much; they live more like a harum-scarum life. Anything coming they grab and what doesn't come they don't make any effort to go after it. A few work too hard and most don't work enough. They want to go to some agency to take care of them and most times they do.

I don't watch television because it's not worth it; I can't hear and to look at it is nothing, silly. I tried putting it up loud, but some of the neighbors said they could hear me across the railroad down there, so I gave it away. I read a lot, mystery stories mostly. I read the *Reader's Digest* and I take about four or five magazines. I love music. I had music lessons when I was eight years old. I bought this organ a few years ago off the trash pile—paid eight dollars for it. I learned a few chords and I have some books that give me the notes. The one thing I wish is that every child in the world, black and white, had access to some musical instrument and a little help in mastering it. You know there are colored people with a rhythm. They have never had the chance I've had and can't get it, but they are doing better now. I can't imagine a home without some musical instrument in it. Another thing I like to do is to identify the birds.

If I had just one good ear I would be doing fine. I take half a fluid pill every morning and a high blood pressure tablet that is to hold the pressure, not to bring it down. I eat well. I like vegetables better than I like meat—I don't like to bite into an animal even if it's cooked—and I have sweets all the time, two or three kinds. I'm in excellent health. My father used to tell me when I was young, "You're too tough to die and too green to burn!"

If I got sick? I'd press a button which sets off an alarm. The sound goes out and the neighbors come in. But I have never used it. If I were ill in bed I wouldn't have to do anything; the neighbors would do it. They would do the right thing. I wouldn't go to a nursing home, not if I can help it. I have friends in a nursing home and I personally detest it. Some people say it is there for your use, but they don't know the bad side. You can't lay a dime down, you can't put a new garment down, somebody will pick it up. It's some of the help, not guests, some of the help. I think they do it in all nursing homes. The food, I don't like it. I couldn't live on it. Soup and sandwiches, soup and sandwiches, that is it, sometimes a cookie. Now then, go over there to that home on X—— Street, you can't walk for walking in human waste on the floor. They don't have enough help lifting those helpless people. I don't know what we need but we need something to keep from going to nursing homes.

The people here in the community, neighbors, we check on each other. This one can look over at that house and she can tell what's going on over there; if the shades are not up by a certain time she goes to see why. If they don't see me in a certain length of time they will come to see why. That neighbor over there came and sat on my porch an hour because she thought I wanted her. Had some painters here and one of them I didn't trust, so she came to stay with me until they were gone. Just little things like that. Long as anybody is well and happy I pay no attention to them, but if they need my help I am there if I can get there. This woman, the second house from here, was called up to Charlotte, her sister was sick. I go over and see if everything is all right and water her flowers, and when her water went off I called her brother and let him come to see why. I check on all the people that I know in the village, if I see anything wrong. I don't have time to go to the new Senior Center, I'm too busy.

Now let me see—we had homecoming at church last week. One day I made two pies and baked fifteen apples, and by that time I am worn out. Next day I cooked a ham and made about forty biscuits, and that's the way my days go all the time. I can't do it all in one day; I have to spread it out. This morning I made a harvest of beets, and this afternoon I have to study my Sunday school lesson. I'm a substitute Sunday school teacher. The lesson is reconciliation and if you can tell me anything about that I wish you would. It's too theological for me. We can't understand how it could take our sins away. I have an idea the preacher couldn't do much with that Sunday school lesson; I know nobody in our class can.

Gladys Hudson · 76 · "Well, I wish there's something... what can I do to help her?"

We met Mrs. Hudson, a tall and trim, white woman, sitting in her favorite rocking chair, an empty coffee can beside her—she dips snuff. Her graying, softly waved, hair is kept neatly arranged under a hairnet. A contented woman, she keeps busy with her sewing and the care of her numerous potted plants. To Mrs. Hudson, home, for the last few years, has been a comfortably furnished trailer on the grounds of her son's house.

My mother and father farmed and I helped them but I've never had a job, nothing other than a housewife. I got married at seventeen and I been married all my life—fifty years—when my husband passed away eight years ago. I got this mobile home and moved up here next to my son two years ago. I enjoy being here so if anything should happen I can run out there or call them and they will be right here. Unless I was very sick, I would stay on here. Should I get very sick, my oldest daughter told me when I moved up here, she says, "Now, Mommy, it's too far for me to come back and forth and if you get sick and can't wait on yourself, you have to come to my house." But we never know what we are going to do—you don't know the future—you just live from day to day.

I got plenty to do. I read—novels, Bible, anything readable I read. I don't care nothing about television, "General Hospital" is about all I ever look at. I travel a lot—back and forth to the children. I mess around here and do little things. If I don't have anything to do, I just walk back and forth through the trailer and through the yard. I don't mind doing anything for anybody. My first cousin's daughter had both her legs amputated and they needed a hospital bed for the home. I don't know what it costs a month to rent a hospital bed, but her mother said she was going need it as long as she lived 'cause she wouldn't never be able to walk nor nothing like that. So they decided they'd buy it. It was going to cost, I believe, $750 to buy. I was sitting here one night and I said, "Well, I wish there's something . . . what can I do to help her?" And I'd been making these little pin cushions, you know, giving them away, and I said, "Well, maybe I can sell them." So my daughter and nieces, different ones, would take them to the hospital and sell them. I gave her eighty-six and a half dollars, and then my little deaf grand-daughter, I gave her some of it. I said she needed help too.

I've got everything I need. The greatest wish I have would be that that little girl right there could hear and talk. That's my youngest granddaughter. She can talk a few words that her mother and daddy can understand, but I can't. That would be my greatest wish. Nobody in this world knows how I worry about that child. I think that she'll make it all right, because deaf people do, but it just does something to me.

Ann Parker · 82 · "My brother said, 'Annie, did anybody ever tell you you didn't have good sense? Anybody work this hard and put up as much [produce]' I says, 'That's my life, don't know when I might find somebody hungry.'"

Mrs. Parker, an erect, energetic, woman with softly wrinkled fair skin and freckles, lives near the Senior Center in Red Hill which opened when she was eighty-five. She attends the center regularly, likes learning new skills in handicrafts and enjoys the companionship the center provides.

Since her husband's death in 1973, she has lived alone in her six-room, white frame house with shingled roof and open front porch. The house is modest but comfortably furnished. Numerous photographs of parents, her husband and herself as newlyweds, children, grandchildren and great grandchildren adorn the walls. The back porch is enclosed and converted into a storeroom for the produce she harvests and puts up. Besides shelves and shelves of bottled tomato juice, jars of stringbeans, pickles and preserves, Mrs. Parker's freezer is packed with corn, butterbeans, peas, okra, and brunswick stew.

Unable to resist feeding people and animals, she is now plagued by the presence of twenty-eight wild cats who live in her garden.

I always lived in a Christian home, and when I was young I felt that anything my father said do was right. I thought he couldn't possibly do anything wrong. The girls had to be boys too and work on the farm, but I didn't object to working one bit. I liked it.

I married when I was nineteen. My husband was a farmer and I helped him till he went to the tobacco factory and worked up there. He come on out here to Red Hill after he retired, but he didn't last too long. He had Parkinson's Disease. I looked after him myself, though I liked to have given up, he was so sick along the last. But I made it and I was happy to have such memories of looking after my father and mother the way I did (they both died in this house in 1930) and then looking after my husband. I lost him but I wanted to stay in my home. I felt I couldn't leave it.

I've done all my own work so far, all my laundry, everything, my sewing, all my housework myself. I don't work very much in the garden now. The man next door tends his garden and mine too. But I gather my vegetables myself. I sit in a folding chair and gather my beans just fine. And I put them up. My brother said to me, "Annie, did anybody ever tell you you didn't have good sense? Anybody work this hard and put up as much [produce] as you've got and nobody but you to eat it." I says, "That's my life, that's what I love; don't know when I might find somebody hungry."

There's things old people need. One thing is to be able to go to the grocery store sometimes. If you had some way of going and carrying several people and let them have a certain day that they was going, then they would have time to do their shopping. My problem is I forget so much and I come back without something I needed, because when I go with someone else I'm always in a hurry and I try to not take up any of their time.

Now, when I go to the Neighborhood Health Center Clinic they do send for me. But you have to wait so long when they carry you over there, and then they have to go off and do something somewhere else.

A checking system for the elderly? Well, it's a good thing. Now, I know a person, you wouldn't say she's elderly, I think she's in her fifties, but she's a little retarded. She lives by herself, and she said to me when her husband got sick and they carried him to her son's house and she had to leave home, she didn't like leaving home. She loved her home and she said, "Mrs. Parker, nobody calls me on the phone, nobody calls me." Well, she's not a person that you would feel like that you just wanted to sit down and have a conversation with, because she's just that much off, but I says, "Mabel, you're not going to say that any longer, because I'm going to call you." And so I make it a habit of calling her. And her daughter tells me that she just looks forward to that and loves it. I've told several neighbors around here, I says, "Listen, we have more time than anything else, let's call people, call people that's shut-in." I feel like they need someone to come round to old people and let 'em know that they're important, that there's no need to just give up and die.

I have a happy life now. I'm not getting too much, but I'm able to live on what I'm getting. Now of course if a spell of sickness come on, I don't know how I could do. I try to not even think about it, I just don't know where I'd go. I have seven children, eighteen grandchildren and twelve great grandchildren. One daughter is sixty years old! I don't know who'd invite me. I don't know who'd do it, this is what I think about.

Sometimes I get to wondering if I know of anybody, that if I got down sick would be willing to come in and help; maybe someone who needed a home. But I hope I never get so sick to go to a nursing home. I hope if I do get that sick, the Lord sees fit to take me away then. But, when I don't think about it, I'll tell you I'm happy. Some people don't want to tell their age, but I don't mind. I'm happy that God has seen fit to keep me here this long. I don't know why He did it, but He has and I'm just glad of it.

Eva Hicks · 74 · "I love dogs. If I had plenty money, honey, I'd have me a pen out here full o' dogs."

Mrs. Hicks, a white woman, lives alone in a seven-room house with a good sized yard, but, because of arthritis she uses only the ground floor. In recent follow-up visits her increasingly stooped posture and wrinkled skin betrayed a fairly rapid aging process. A very friendly, pleasant person, she hardly ever leaves her home because she doesn't like to leave her animals—two dogs and two cats.

When I was born they didn't even put down births. I reckon my last birthday was the fifteenth of April—I'm seventy-four years old. I was raised in a cotton mill. In my young days, my childhood, there warn't enough people to run this mill. So they took little children, ten, twelve years old—they liked the job and they did it. I could spool, spin, and do anything in there. My daddy was a railroad man and then he served as policeman fifteen years, and then along towards the last he was a spare hand in the mill.

My sister and I get together and relive that life, the old days. We had a big time. There was a big crowd of us and I think the bigger the family is the happier they are. We didn't have everything like the children has now, but our mommy raised us. You know people now have them and somebody else raise them—ain't that right? Our father use to tell us every week, "Now trim your fingernails every Friday and you won't never have the toothache." We all had to keep our shoes clean, he checked 'em every night. We had a nice mommy and daddy. They raised us to work, we all had a job to do. For fun we would make a playhouse. It warn't like children now with bicycles, doll babies. People don't fix now so the children will enjoy Christmas. We had Christmas onc't a year and we enjoyed Christmas. I went to school, too, but honey, I just went up to the fifth grade. I think the old times was better. We didn't have this push-button stuff, and we didn't have bathrooms but we was happy. Now the world is in a hurry, everybody's got more than they can do. I'm like the old sun. Takes me back to yesterday onc't more.

I am shame to tell you how long I was married. I warn't quite sixteen when I married, and I just lost my husband three years ago this past July. We stayed together fifty-seven years. Honey, I had a good husband. To me he goes right on living! I had five children. My three girls is dead and I got two boys living. My last girl had polio, the oldest one died of T.B., my baby died at birth. You know girls are much better to momma and daddy. I wish it had been the Lord's will to have let one of my girls live. I have one boy living in Greensboro and one in Mill Town. I see one son sometimes every week, just different times. My sister from Virginia comes and spends months at the time with me and cleans and mows the yard. She can crank that mower up like a man. When she's not here I have two little colored boys to help in the yard. I got one of the best colored neighbors down here; him and his wife are just as smart as they can be. But, Lord, nobody helps me clean the house. I do it all by myself. And I love to cook. I still make biscuits every morning.

When I need to go to the doctor I go to the clinic right here. They come and pick me up. The biggest pull back we old women out here have is going shopping for our groceries. I cain't drive. It's one big mistake I made, but it's too late now. I think I'm too old to learn. I sold my husband's car and I wish though sometimes, I had a kept it and got in that thing and learned. I used to drive long time ago when you didn't have to have a driver's license.

I live on Social Security. When my check comes I have to go to the bank and put money in there to pay my light bills, my phone bill, and my insurance. What I have left I have to buy groceries. I don't buy no clothes; I don't need 'em 'cause I don't go nowhere. Honey, I have to live on a budget. I have to pay tax on this place, I got to have my oil drum filled up, but I try to manage. Even if I had food stamps, or could get food stamps, I couldn't get to go get 'em. A nurse came out and talked to me about that when my husband first died. I told her I thought I could manage without 'em. It looks like you get such a little with 'em anyway—you don't get very much. My son help me out in my grocery bill 'cause he has a big deep freeze and he puts up all he can.

When my friend across the road died I run an ad in the paper for someone to come live with me, but no one come. Long time ago you could get a good ol' colored woman would come and live with you. Be glad to have a private home. You take these rest homes now—it's took over; I think they has caused things being like it is. But, honey, as long as I can get up and wait on myself, I thank the Lord. I keep myself busy. I always try to find something to do. I crochet in the winter and I read a right much: I like history and I try to read my Bible some everyday, and I get the evening paper.

I get awful lonesome, though, sometimes. But I work in my flowers. I got four or five ol' chickens, I tend to 'em. I trim my hedges, tend to both of my dogs. I love dogs. I got one out here, my yard dog, the one I keep tied. He ain't got sense, that one. When he gets a loose, he's gone; it's 'cause he stays tied. The other one is Rickie. She sleeps at the foot of my bed every night, unless she get hot, and then she get down and get up in the big ol' chair there. Rickie was ten last November. I had a male cocker spaniel and he lived to get fifteen or sixteen years old. When he died I grieved over him so much and missed him, my grandson gave me Rickie for a Christmas present. I got dog food but she eats mostly what I eat, eggs, bacon, buttered bread.

But Rickie got sick, it'll be three years this Christmas. She was in season and she kept a spotting and a discharge and I knowed something was wrong. I called the vet, and he said, "Well, Mrs. Hicks, have her here by nine o'clock if you can." So, I didn't know what to do, so I called my son and says, "Son, I got to go to the doctor and take my dog." I says, "She's really sick." He says, "Well, Mama, as soon as I report down at my job, I'll be out there to take you." So you know what he told his bossman? "I've got to go take my mama to the doctor." He didn't tell no certain doctor, you know. Just says, "I got to go take my mama to the doctor."

We had Rickie over there by nine fifteen. Old Dr. ——— looked her over and checked her over and he says, "Nothing to do but operate, Mrs. Hicks." I says, "Lord, Dr. ———, Rickie's too old for that." He says, "Now you go home and get that ol' broom and get busy. And you stay busy all day today. And I'm going let you hear from Rickie at four o'clock." So my son come in here after lunch and laid down on the couch. He says, "Mama," he says, "I ain't going back home 'cause we got to go back to the doctor's office and get Rickie." So I got him up fifteen minutes to four. I says, "The doctor knows as much now as he'll know in fifteen minutes, call him." I was just so upset over my dog I didn't know what to do. So he called, and Dr. ——— said Rickie was ready to come home. When I got there, I put her on a leash. And you know, she went out the door and saw that car and she slipped a loose from me and run and jumped in the front seat!

I would like to get another puppy, another cocker spaniel. Rickie won't like a puppy around. Honey, she is just as jealous of my grand-children. When the little ones are here, she will get around behind me and stick her head under my arm, move my hand. I love dogs. When my husband was living he was a carpenter before he retired. After he retired he raised beagle hounds, hunting dogs. One time we had eigh-teen dogs here, puppies and all! He raised 'em and he sold 'em. That was his enjoyment, his pleasure, and I went along with it. If I had plenty money, honey, I'd have me a pen out here full o' dogs.

loneliness

"If you know some nice widow
that would like to marry me"

Will Clark · 67 · "Dear friend, I want to ask you a favor. If you know some nice widow that would like to marry me, let me know."

Mr. Clark, tall and thin, has a pronounced limp due to a fall from a ladder while painting his house in 1972. His long, deeply lined face has an almost grayish tinge, which, added to a generally somber mien, projects a feeling of dejection and depression. He wears his late wife's dental plate, because his own plate was broken at the time of his accident. A deeply religious white man, he has been deacon of his church for more than twenty years and teaches in the Sunday school.

Mr. Clark's white frame, four-room house is set back by a small expanse of grass from a paved country road. A flowering vine covers the trellis on the front porch; several flower beds and a vegetable patch are behind the house.

Once a successful farmer with modest savings, Mr. Clark's savings were consumed by medical bills for his wife and son, now both dead. His Social Security ($78 a month in 1973) is now spent almost entirely on his own doctors' bills, medications and health insurance.

I been by myself five years since my wife died. She had cancer and stayed in the hospital for three months. Then I had to carry her back every day for six straight weeks for the cobalt treatment. Then she got taken bad again and went back to the hospital for three months 'fore she died. I lost my only son with lung cancer and had to look out for his five children. It just run me down to nothing. I had cancer insurance but my wife didn't. Insurance paid $5,000 of the hospital bill. It took everything I could scratch out and get my hands on to finish paying off the rest—$14,000. Took me three years to pay it off. Now I get food stamps. If it wasn't for that I couldn't live. And my two daughters help me out a little.

After I paid off the hospital bill, I took to arthritis and then started bleeding from my ulcers again and stayed in the hospital the biggest portion of a month. I been going to the doctor onc't or twic't a month ever since. It takes just 'bout everything I get out of Social Security. Social welfare, they help me out some on my medical bills. Anything I worked I made good at, but the money went out faster than I made it. Hospital and doctor bills. I had three operations in one year.

The main thing that I need is someone to stay by me. I would just like to be 'round somebody sometime for company. My wife was an angel. I was sixteen and she was seventeen when we married. We 'bout raised ourselves together. She was good and happy, wore a smile all the time. She would take food out of her own mouth and give it to any child that needed it. We stuck side-by-side, day in and day out, worked together on the farm.

My family come to see me on Sunday afternoons. I go to church Sunday mornings. The good Lord been good to me. If He hadn't, I wouldn't be here today. Never night nor morning goes over my head that my prayers don't go with me, and 'fore I lay down at night.

Shortly after this first visit and interview in 1975, in response to a Christmas card I sent him, Will Clark wrote me this letter. I have put in some punctuation and changed some spelling but have not altered the substance of the letter:

1/12/76

Dear friend, will answer your sweet letter with best wishes and a Happy New Year. Appreciated you all's visit. I am getting on fine and I want to ask you a favor. If you know some nice widow that would like to marry me and share my nice home and flowers and housekeep, I would love for you to let me know. My phone number is ———. Have anyone to call after 6 P.M. Any age from forty to sixty-five years old would be great. Thanks of you. Will talk to anyone.

Yours truly and best wishes,
Will Clark
Ashton, N. C.

Nice home for anyone and flowers

I replied as follows:

1/28/76

Dear Mr. Clark,

Thank you for your nice letter and greetings. I think the best way to meet a nice lady that would want to marry you is for you to meet people in a group.

I have made some inquiries and the nearest group of senior citizens is at the ——— center. They meet in the ——— church on ——— road every day, Monday through Friday, from 10 A.M. to 2 P.M.

A hot lunch is served daily and you pay what you can afford. It could be as little as twenty-five cents. Or you can give food stamps.

*You can go there or you can call Mrs. —— telephone ——. I'm told
that it is a very nice group and I'm sure you will meet good people.
Do let me know how you find the group.*

Best Wishes,
Eva J. Salber

*A visit to Mr. Clark in 1977 found him depressed after a bout in the
hospital with pneumonia, and a visit in 1979 found him still single,
but beginning to be interested in a woman he had met and befriended
seven or eight years earlier.*

*A visit in the fall of 1980 revealed a smiling, rejuvenated man wear-
ing newly acquired dentures. Three weeks previously, he had married
a woman of forty-six, divorced, with a thirteen-year-old child.*

She was an old friend I met at Mill Town Hospital. She was there for
a check-up and I was there for a check-up. Her little daughter who was
with her needed a skin graft. Her husband had left home, and she didn't
have a thing in this world. I said, "God bless your heart, you don't have
a place to stay the night." And I got her a place to stay and it ain't cost
her a penny. And I done forgot her. That was almost ten years ago.

I seen her two or three times over the years when she'd write me a
letter and tell me she'd have to bring the child back to the bospital. I'd
meet her there.

Four years ago she separated from her husband and then they got
divorced. And 'bout a year ago she wrote to tell me she was divorced. I
wrote her back and she said it looks like we going to have to get
together.

So that's it, and we married three weeks ago. She stayed down here
week 'fore last, cleaned up the house and everything in the world I got.
She's coming back tomorrow and I'll leave with her sometime next
week to where she's got a place to live at. I'm leaving my house to
my daughters—lease it to them now—and they'll give me enough to
live on.

She thinks the world of me. She said, "You're a God loving man,
you're a lot older than I am, but you're the person I'm looking for."
She's forty-six years old; I'll show you her picture, she favors my first
wife. [The picture showed a plump, good looking, smiling woman and
was inscribed, "Love you, Will for everlasting till the end."] She's a
religious lady, and no two-way question 'bout it. She's got a heart of
gold. I hope and pray to God that you can meet her.

I sat at this table to eat by myself for the past nine years, and I done
got tired of it. It seemed like the end of the world was at hand. So I

made a decision. I been to a lot of doctors, but since this come up and I met this lady ten years ago and come back in contact with her and married her, she done me more good than every doctor that I've ever been to yet with the happiness and pleasure that I haven't seen for years, and it done me more good than all the medicine ever I took. I feel just as good as I felt when I was fifty years old.

Donald Phillips · 76 · "The worst thing after my wife died was being to yourself, I reckon, and missing her too. Tbe Saturday 'fore she died we'd been married for forty-eight years."

Mr. Phillips is very tall and gaunt. His muscles show some wasting, his back is stooped, his gait slow and deliberate. His fair skin, tanned from outdoor exposure, looks weathered rather than healthy.

The two-story farm house he lives in belongs to his nephew and is well cared for. Simply, and rather sparsely, furnished, it is kept spotless by an elderly black man who works part-time on the farm.

When we came to see him, a year after our first visit, Mr. Phillips had recently returned from the hospital where he had undergone a hernia operation. Still feeling the effects of the operation, and needing to keep warm, he was very worried at the rising cost of fuel oil that cold winter. One hundred dollars a month of his Social Security check of $180 had gone towards keeping him warm.

My wife's nephew owns this land, the house too. I pay him $60 a month rent. 'Course I ain't got it. I got to catch that up now. I don't own a thing in the world but an old pick-up truck. I farmed three-quarters shares, and I furnished my own equipment till my wife died two years ago. I quit farming soon after then. I didn't have nobody to cook or to help me, and my daughter was dead too. The worst thing after my wife died was being to yourself, I reckon, and missing her too. The Saturday 'fore she died we'd been married for forty-eight years. It was a poor home but it was a good one.

Now I ain't suffering for something to eat. I cook for myself, and I take a lot of exercise. I get out here and work in the yard. Don't watch T.V. too much since my wife died. I like the wrestling the best but I just don't care a thing about it since she died. 'Fore she died, me and her this time of the year would always eat kind of early and come in here and turn on the T.V. and set some nights till after eleven o'clock. I just sits here now and look at my paper and fall back and go to doze. Once in a while I turn it on. Sometimes I visit my sister's daughter. I don't do too much visiting here in the community. You see, everybody's busy and I don't want to bother them. I been thinking about going to the Senior Center you told me about but I couldn't go 'cause I ain't got nobody to keep my clothes in shape to go nowhere, and I just have to do the best I can. I ain't had the money to carry them and have them cleaned and laundered.

I don't like to stay here on the place right by myself, but I have to. It's lonely. Then, you know, it's getting sort of dangerous for anybody to stay to themselves now, day or night. You see in the paper everyday what happens around, so much meanness. My nephew and his wife say they going to look after me as long as I live, but I don't want to be that much burden on nobody.

I reckon the best time was when my daughter and my wife's niece was at home. They was just small girls and following me around. I reckon that was the best time ever I seen in my life.

Well, I'm thankful I'm in the shape I'm in and able to get around. Because there's a lot of people a whole lot younger than I am that cain't get around and ain't able to do nothing. I think that comes from the way they eat a whole lot, exposing theyselves to the weather, losing a lot of sleep. I was never nobody that lost a lot of sleep. I got a doctor. I thought I had a heart attack last August, so the colored fellow called my nephew, and the ambulance come and carried me to the hospital. The doctor have me a check-up and he told me that I was in good a shape for my age as anybody that he had seen. He told me not to come back unless I needed him. So I ain't thought I needed him, so I ain't been back. I don't take no medicine or nothing but a BC or aspirin once in a while.

Didn't go to school much. We'd go three or four days and would have to quit and work or something. I never did get no education; I just went some until I was about fourteen years old. Not enough to do me no good. After my daddy died—I was about twenty-one years old—I went to Mill Town and went to work and I learnt more on the job than I ever learnt at school. I couldn't hardly read and write my name 'fore I went. I worked at Warner Cotton Mill—tore bed sheets and I walked and slid together the length of that bed sheet—108 inches long, and I had to walk and slide the lengths together. I had to tear four thousand a day, and they paid you $1.25 a thousand. I was telling some of the young boys here a while back what I worked on for a week—they called it piece work. They laughed at me. They said they wouldn't have worked any at all. I worked there from about 1920 for three years for $14.96 a week, fifty-six hours a week.

My mother left me 'fore I married and went to stay with her brother. She had two brothers that was bachelors. I went to my aunt and boarded till I was married. That is how I come to be married I reckon; if my mother had stayed with me I don't reckon I would've married. After my sister married my mother got grannyfied, and she wanted to leave town to be with the grandbabies. I lived in Mill Town the first two years I was married. My daughter was born and her health got kind of bad and we wanted to get back out in the country. So I moved out here and I've been here ever since. I went back to farming and I've been farming ever since—about fifty years—till I wasn't able any more.

Yes, I caught it tough all my life. My daddy was paralyzed from a stroke when I was seven and I took his place on the farm for fourteen years till he died. And I lost my wife and my daughter. But I still enjoy living. I see a lot of pleasure in sitting around here and watching the traffic come to the road. There's a whole lot of things a body can amuse theyselves. And there's a whole lot to be thankful for. I'm thankful to be living, looking around to see the flowers and the crops growing, thankful that I can get around as good as I can. I'd like to live a hundred years if I could.

Bill Hall · 81 · "I'll tell you the truth, it's so lonely, I catch myself to speaking to her."

Mr. Hall is slightly stooped, but still a handsome man with fair complexion and clear blue eyes. His hands are tremulous and his gait unsteady; he walks with a cane but continues to tend the garden. His hearing and vision are good and he enjoys drawing on his excellent memory in reminiscing about the past. His simple, green cement-block house across the road from his daughter's house, has a well equipped kitchen containing an electric stove, refrigerator, and a freezer kept amply stocked by his children.

Mr. Hall owns a pick-up truck but now confines his driving to the local area.

I been married going on fifty-three years when my wife died. I been a knowing her ever since she was nothing but a kid, 'fore we was married. We had just as great a marriage, I reckon, as anybody that ever lived. There ain't no doubt 'bout that. I don't care if I's to get up at midnight to carry a load of 'bacco, she'd roll right out and have me something to eat 'fore I left the house. Sometimes, I'd get up and carry off a load so I could sell that day and get back the same day, and I never left without eating. And curing 'bacco—I had to tend to it all night by myself. She'd kill a chicken and fix me something for a midnight snack. She'll be dead three years the tenth of this coming February. It's been awful lonesome. I'll tell you the truth, it's so lonely, I catch myself to speaking to her, 'cause she usually sit right here and I'd sit over there in that chair.

After the first week she died, I ain't never slept in the bedroom—I sleep out here on this roll-away bed.

When my wife was living there was someone out here all the time. But when a man's wife's gone there ain't nobody don't come round much. And I miss that. I do have lots of kin to come visit me though. They're here every year before Christmas, for Christmas dinner, just like my wife fixed. She said that there's so many of 'em she couldn't give 'em all a present 'cause she didn't have money enough to buy for all of 'em, and they said, "Well, we'd rather have a Christmas dinner than to have all the presents you can give us." Now I'll tell you, my wife'd spend $50 or $75 for stuff to cook and she enjoyed it better than anything in the world, and she was one more cook and she didn't use a recipe to cook nothing. Nary daughter I got can cook like she can, and they'll tell you they couldn't cook like their mama. They come here every Christmas day, to my house, and we have dinner right here. They bring some, and some of 'em come in and cook here. There's about thirty or forty each year.

During 'bacco season I work some in the fields with my son, Tom. Through the summer I do just hoe work to help Tom out some. I go out to the field after breakfast and work with him and his two girls a couple hours and then I go down to my regular work. Grading eggs. It ain't hard work, but it's hard on the feet and knees walking them cement floors. I've picked up and counted as high as 15,400 eggs in some six hours and a half.

I don't take a dose of medicine but for the diabetic capsules. You see, when I stayed up there working in the chicken-house, sometimes you'd have water to drink and sometimes, in the winter, you didn't have it 'cause it stayed froze up half the time. So I drunk so many o' these Coca Colas—I always liked a Coca Cola—that the doctor said I had the diabetic. So he put me on a diet for two weeks and he give me them diabetic capsules to take. After that the diabetic ain't never showed on me since, and I can eat anything in the world I want to eat. I told my doctor I was going quit taking them capsules. He wouldn't say quit and he wouldn't say keep on, so I miss taking 'em a day or two along at times but I still take 'em, one a day. It's been about five years. I get 'em every time they give out; I send and get me some more. All I have to do is just carry the bottle; they refill it every time I carry it down there.

I buy 'bacco when I want it. I've never suffered for nothing. I buy what I want and pay for it, and I don't buy that which I don't need. I'm right fortunate—with my little Social Security check, I get nearly $400 a month now, and me a working. I make near 'bout that. I ain't going promise about going back to work no more. I've got enough to live on without it, not bragging at all. But I'd rather to do something than to do nothing. I just feel better at it. Something to look forward to.

Rose Chambers · 82 · "When I leave here you know where I want to go? To the cemetery."

Mrs. Chambers, short, plump, with sloping shoulders and bowed back, walks with some difficulty holding onto furniture for support. Her thinning gray hair is drawn back from a broad forehead into a bun. Dark bushy eyebrows lend strength to her pale face with its softly rounded, sagging cheeks.

She owns her single-story frame house which is beginning to show signs of deterioration. The floorboards of the front porch, decorated with bright potted plants, are rotting and hazardous. Her living room is small and crowded; it would be easy to stumble against the oil heater. There is an indoor bathroom with toilet, but no grips on the bathtub. Mrs. Chambers can no longer get in and out of the bath and washes herself sitting on the edge of the tub. A handmade patchwork quilt covers her bed, and family photographs are much in evidence in living and dining rooms. The house, warm, cheerful, and neat is modestly but comfortably furnished. Mrs. Chambers, proud of her handiwork, showed us a trunkful of quilts which she keeps in her "plunder [storage] room."

Way back when we was coming up, we had a good time and didn't know it. We didn't have no responsibilities. We lived on the farm and do what we was told to do, plant corn, chop corn, we didn't care. We pick up our hoe and go to the field. We worked hard but we was use to it. We lived for years right close to a railroad. That was back when the passenger trains was running. We never was too busy what we wouldn't stop to see that train come by. I miss them old trains. We had plenty to eat and no responsibility. Now we have plenty to eat but it's so high.

I was twenty-three when I got married. If Walter had lived till the fifth of April—he died the third of February—we'd have been together fifty-three years. He use to say how long we'd lived together and we hadn't had a fight yet. He was sick a long time 'fore he died. He had leukemia and he was in and out of the hospital for ten years. The worst thing is missing him. He died on a Saturday evening and he was buried on Monday. It just seemed like a dream to me. I didn't do a thing in the world, I knew somebody was here all the time helping me—my sister, my brother, my niece, the two foster children we brought up.

I still work in the yard but I don't have no garden now. I cain't hold out to work in it. But I have something to do all the time. I mop the floors, I sweep, I do my washing, I do my ironing, I do my cooking. I piece up bed quilts. I use to do a whole lot of embroidery but I ain't done none of that in seven years. I got to have my glasses changed but I ain't been yet. I got to save up a little more money 'fore I can do that. Everything's so high.

I get Social Security, $134 and I get $36.36 on the gold check [SSI]. If it wasn't for Social Security, I wouldn't be here. No, I ain't never got no food stamps. What money I get I make it go. When I first get my check I'll pay my phone bill and light bill. Then I buy my oil and a little wood. It's hard to save up enough to have my glasses changed.

I have high blood and I had a light stroke on my left side two years ago. It left my hand and foot cold and a curious feeling on this left side. The doctor tells me not to eat no more pork and stay off the salt. I get me a pound of sausage and I will cook me a cake every other day now, sometimes three days along. If I feel all right I still make biscuits once a day.

My twin brother [George Ross] wanted me to come up yonder and stay with him after his second daughter died. Just this house and what I got in the house is all I got, and I didn't want to be shutting up what I had and go up there. I told him to come down here and stay with me. No, he wanted to stay at home. I said, "I do, too." I am doing pretty good here by myself but I miss Walter still. When I leave here you know where I want to go? To the cemetery.

the burdens of illness

"Medicine is so high"

Virginia Ferrell · 86 · "I wish I could talk better. I don't know what caused that trouble. Dr. S ——, that's my doctor, he never mentioned one thing about my voice, and he's been my doctor since '46."

A short, thin, stooped white woman with gray hair and wrinkled skin, Mrs. Ferrell is physically frail but mentally sharp and alert. Despite failing vision, deafness, and partial paralysis of her vocal cords, which hindered the flow of conversation, she enjoyed talking with us during our interviews and was decidedly loquacious.

Her six-room frame house, situated next door to the home of her only surviving son, is in sound condition and has indoor plumbing. Mrs. Ferrell manages by herself during the daytime, but sleeps in her son's house at night. In addition to her failing vision and deafness, the onset of heart failure made spending nights alone inadvisable.

R. T. (he's my son) just come in a while ago, brought in my Social Security check, $82. Well, I handed it back to him for him to get it cashed out here. R. T. doesn't farm, he works at the tobacco company in Mill Town. I stay in his house all night. R. T. gets up, he fixes some coffee, brings me on home and I cook breakfast, dinner and supper, just like I always did, but not as much.

I ain't got no money. Medicine is so high. Look here, seven bottles of medicine. This one, I take every morning, and this, I believe it's three times a day. I cain't quite make it out—I need new glasses. But I know which ones to take. When I come from up yonder, I'll straighten 'em out, set 'em on the kitchen table so I can pick 'em up. You have to keep on the look-out, and it does worry you, though, I'll tell you that. Pick up the wrong thing, set it back down and pick up something else. They all got Dr. S ——'s name on 'em. That one cost $11.81 and R. T.'s going to get some of that this evening. I paid near about $12 for that one that I takes one a day. I pay for it all myself. I don't know how old folks like us are going to keep on living if medical costs keep going up.

I wish I could talk better. I don't know what caused that trouble. When I'd have a bad cold, all after I got up some size, I'd have a little of this trouble. But this thing's been going on about four years, and a getting worse. Some mornings I get up, I'm all right, then again, before night I'm not. Dr. S ——, that's my doctor, he never mentions one thing about my voice, and he's been my doctor since '46. I'm going to ask him what causes that. I think he's wonderful. He told me the other day, he said, "You haven't got this, you haven't got that, you haven't got that." He didn't call no name, but he said nothing's giving me trouble at my age, but my heart. My daughter-in-law, R. T.'s wife, takes me to see him. Used to take myself in the old car, and I'm ashamed to tell you why I quit driving. They've got a grown boy and he just wanted my car every little bit, so I give him my car. I didn't want to go nowhere.

I was two years old when my mama died. My daddy lived nine years after she died and all of us children stayed on the farm till we got grown. I was the baby. Part of my life's been good and part of it's been terrible bad; so, course, the good part is the best and you hope the bad don't come no more, but it comes. I believe everybody has a little bad luck. Even if they millionaires, I believe they have some bad luck, don't you? Sometimes, I just burst out into crying. Sometimes, I laugh. Sometimes, I sing. I cain't sing now, though. Well, all I know to say is make the best of the worst and keep going.

I forget how long my husband's been dead—about fourteen years, I reckon. He was a coal man 'fore they built this lake down here. They got that running and he didn't haul no more coal. We bought this place and he just rented the farm out and done whatever he pleased. I've lived down here by myself now four years. I stay down here in the daytime. That's my son, R. T.'s, house out there and like I told you I stay out there at night. Stayed here by myself after Will died four years, but you don't know how things will get.

If I get so as I cain't stay here by myself, I'd go to R. T.'s. I don't have nowhere else to go. R. T. was supposed to take care of me and his daddy as long as we lived. That's how come Will give the children a acre to build 'em a house on.

I had three children. Betty's dead and gone, the baby boy that lived in Virginia's dead and gone, and my husband's dead and gone. Nobody but me and R. T. But I have a lot of people, widow women like me, come and spend the week with me.

I have a bathroom in here. That spigot in the toilet needs fixing. R. T.'s tried one man about four weeks; he promise to come here one night, then he promise to come if we let him work on Sunday. When I use that toilet, I have to draw water out of the kitchen and carry it in there. I take a shower, get in that bath then I pull the curtain and I can stay under there as long as I want to. R. T. sends my wash to the laundry, but I wash my best dress and things myself.

You know what I'm doing? I'm fixing over that old dress I washed. I'm wearing my use-to-be Sunday dresses. I said I'm going to wear my old Sunday clothes for everyday and buy me some Sunday ones. But I'm

108

not going to pack the closet full, 'cause I ain't got that much money and I won't live much longer as old as I am. I cain't!

The worst thing about getting old is that you got to work like a dog. Work all the time. I've got a lot of things that I had to quit, though. I use to tend to that whole garden. I use to sell all the garden down at the farmers' market. Well, since there's nobody here but me, I don't work like I use to. I cain't. I've given up my garden, I've sold all my chickens, I've sold my cow and calf. Now, I'm not lying, but I owned this plantation. When me and my husband are both dead, R. T. gets the plantation, but it's mine as long as I live. And that's a lot of trouble. A lot of expense. If you don't live on a farm, you better be glad of it. I have tried but I couldn't get it farmed. People are working on public work. They don't want to farm. They want their money every Friday now.

Beulah Perry · 88 · "I am contented with my life. I have to be. So many people think the world owes them somebody to take care of them, but I don't. I don't think anybody owes me anything."

Mrs. Perry's face is pale and wrinkled and her gray eyes are almost hidden from view behind the thick lenses of her glasses. Her limited vision necessitates the use of a cane in walking. Much of her day is spent resting on a reclining chair.

Her husband had been relatively prosperous, owning his own farm, a store and a filling station. When he died, a son took over the management of the estate and has ensured his mother's continued comfort. She lives in a one-story, six-room brick house which overlooks the main highway from Ashton. It is in excellent condition, is equipped with all modern amenities and is comfortably furnished. A young couple, who live rent free in a trailer on Mrs. Perry's land, shop and prepare her meals.

A neighbor, describing her, says: "Mrs. Perry has an interest in everybody in this community, black and white. She's the backbone and stabilizing force in the community. I come two, maybe three, times a week to read the Bible to her and deal with her personal correspondence. She said to me not long ago, "I want to finish the Bible before I pass on," and I answered that we would. We've finished Genesis, Exodus, Leviticus, Numbers, Deuteronomy—now we're in Joshua. She's just remarkable. She taught at the little church up there;

she taught children and grandchildren at the Sunday school. I could write a book on her."

My husband died twenty years ago and four years later I gave my lifetime right to a part of my land to a young couple. They live in a trailer near my house and I see them every day. I pay them $60 a month to cook and bring me food.

I can't see well, so I can't fix what I eat. That's why I was telling you that you would have to fix the food yourself if you wanted to stay and have lunch with me. Three times a day they bring my food. When they want to go fishing or off somewhere, they bring me a sandwich or something that I can open up and eat by myself. When they go to Florida in the winter for about three months, my granddaughter cooks for me. She's liable to get married anytime, but one of the neighbors said that she'd come then. So I try not to worry.

My children say I don't eat enough to keep a bird alive and I don't eat right, because I eat mostly starches, but I've lived to be eighty-eight! When they fuss with me about eating I say, "Well, I'm here. I'll bet you all don't stay here that long."

I have a colored girl who comes and does housecleaning. She's the sweetest thing. She lived with me when she was fourteen; my sons were little boys then. She's real nice, never has failed to come. She will come anytime, take me to see my neighbors when she gets through cleaning and helping me get my bath. I can't get in the bath if I am here by myself. I'm alone at night but I sleep very well and I'm not afraid, haven't got sense enough I reckon!

A friend of mine who lives by herself [Virginia Ferrell] worries me to death; she wants me to come and live with her. I can't do that. I'm too well situated here. But I need to have someone come and stay with me if I can get them. I've advertised, but everyone that came were all worse off sick than I was! You can't seem to get anybody to live with you. I guess the government takes care of them. That's why I built this house sixteen years ago with two baths, one in my room and another for people who would come to care for me, but I haven't been able to get anyone.

Now, if I get disabled, I would have to go to the hospital first. Course I'd have my doctor to see what was wrong with me, then they would recommend a nursing home, I reckon. I just don't want to go to a nursing home though. They treat them bad they say. Most old people, their mind isn't good at all. Mrs. Morgan went to a rest home and some neighbors went over there to see her. They had her tied in a chair and she slipped down about half way; was hanging there. So her daughter of fifty-eight quit her job and went to tend to her mother in the afternoons so as to give her her evening meal. Now, Flower Manor over here, my husband's cousin's wife is there now and she hollers "Help! Help!" all the time they say. She just doesn't know what she's doing. I couldn't rest in a home where everybody was hollering and carrying on. I have it so quiet here.

Two ladies from this community have been here to help me, and they say they want to come back. I hope they will come. One could stay eight hours—she has a husband—the other one lives alone. She wants to look at T.V., doesn't have a T.V., and wants to look at mine. I don't want them as companions, I want them to come and cook for me and stay here.

I was just thinking about how I was going to spend Thanksgiving. Being thankful I reckon. I don't have much the matter with me at all. At Mill Town Hospital they tell me it's nothing but old age. I thought that two of my sons were going to come for Thanksgiving—they have their own business—but they only can take off one day, so it wasn't worth it to come from Kansas City and Miami here for one night and day. My son that lives up here took over the land and farm when my husband died. But I'm not going to spend Thanksgiving with him. I have right nice daughters-in-law but they are not my own daughters. I don't know how it would be with a daughter, but I feel like I could go stay with a daughter if I had one.

I have plenty of visitors. They are young and don't stay very long. Yesterday my son and my granddaughter came and we had breakfast together. If I don't have visitors, honey, I just lean back and be thankful. I don't know how I get through the day and the night, but I have done very well I think. I don't watch television very much; the old stories are so dirty, but you can't find nothing else to look at. And I can't read. I haven't been able to read now for four years, not even a word, not even my own name. The doctors don't know why. Old age they say. Said it was film over my eyes getting thicker. I hope I don't go blind before I have to go, but when I have to go it's all right. I wasn't always ready to go, but I'm ready now. I would be just as happy in one place as another.

Honey, I'm so much better off if I have company. I really think I need somebody with me, but they charge so much just to sit and look at you. And there's so few old people that worked and saved their money when they were getting a dollar a day or a dollar and a half where they get twenty now. They want so much money and I just can't pay that much.

Of course my children would pay if I asked them, but I don't want them to do it. I get good Social Security. I never did work any; I just get my husband's. Having a home of my own and my son taking care of it and paying the taxes and everything, I really don't have too much to do with money, don't have to spend much. When my husband died twenty years ago, he left everything to me as long as I live, but I just turned it all over to the boys.

I manage pretty well. I have a porch out there that used to be my garage. I had that wired in and an indoor-outdoor rug put on it. I walk out there sometimes one hundred and fifty times a day—one hundred and fifty times from one corner to the other. I have a rod I hold to keep from falling. Till a few years ago I drove my car, and I still drove to Florida when I was eighty. Then I gave the car to one of my granddaughters because I couldn't see too good. I've been to Miami nearly every year. I get homesick when I think about it. They want me to come but I don't want to go anywhere, anymore.

There are organizations out here that arrange activities for people. They had a supper for the senior citizens, as they designate us, on Sunday afternoon at Ashton. I told them that I couldn't come; I don't like to get in a crowd; most of them are younger than I am, so much younger. I still belong to our church club that I started about fifty or sixty years ago, The Christian Women's Society. But, I don't want to go there anymore; I just keep my membership paid up. This lady that comes and plays Canasta with me, she reads the Sunday school lesson to me every week.

I am contented with my life. I have to be. So many people think the world owes them somebody to take care of them, but I don't. I don't think anybody owes me anything. My children were the best children. My son in Kansas calls me every morning. He says he doesn't smoke or drink so it doesn't cost as much as a pack of cigarettes. I was telling somebody the other day the reason I live so long is because my children are so good. They are the nicest boys.

Ella Daniels · 72 · "My case worker sent me a reading machine—they got so many gadgets and levers—I just couldn't operate it—and sent it back to them."

A strong, protruding lower jaw gives Mrs. Daniels' pale face an appearance of strength and determination in spite of sightless, sunken eyes.

She is stockily built, her arthritic knees restrict her walking and give her severe pain. She lives in a deteriorating frame house; the boards on the front porch are broken, the stairs rickety and unsafe. She reports that the owner told her she would "just have to get used to those stairs."

At each of our several visits, Mrs. Daniels, who regularly dips snuff, sat on a plain wooden chair in her bedroom, a spitoon can conveniently placed beside her.

My husband died the thirteenth day of February 1973, and I've been left alone since then. But my sister stays with me at night—been going on three years now—'cause my vision is bad and she don't want me to stay here at night alone.

My vision's been bad ever since I was seventeen years old. I cain't see you plain; you look more or less like a shadow. But it has not been as bad as it is now. See, I had two operation transplants on this eye; I went to Johns Hopkins when my baby boy was in service. My home doctor advised me to go, because he had an operation there and it was wonderful. And so I went and the doctor, he took the stitches out on the fourteenth day, and right there he told me not to blink my eye and I couldn't help from blinking. That made him mad and he says, "I bet you a damn dollar I do get that stitch out," and made it bleed and broke the transplant a loose and it went bad. That's what happened to me. I went for the best but I got the worst.

My case worker sent me a reading machine so I could get my choice of books to read, and did you know they have changed them? I had one a long time go and that was the easiest to operate. All you had to do was to plug it in and put your book on and turn it on; it'd start reading to you. I learnt a lot from the Bible with that machine reading to me. They've changed them now, and they've got so many gadgets and levers and this and that I just couldn't operate it. My son visited—and he knows a lot about electric appliances—and he couldn't get it going, so I had to get my mail carrier to come to the house and pick it up and sent it back to them. I told them not to send me another because they had changed them, and I was afraid I'd never learn to operate it.

My marriage was not too good, a girl makes a mistake sometimes. My husband had drinking problems. That's something I ain't never craved in my life and I thank God for it. I don't like drinking. He had fits for nothing, I didn't give him no cause. It looked like it was bred and born in him to fight. When he said he was going to fight me I told him that if he did he'd better make a sure thing of it, because if he hit me to hurt me and if I lived, then he would never hit nobody else because I was going to put him out of business. We stayed together almost forty-eight years. I couldn't leave him on account of my vision. Life was very hard then.

Didn't have no fun. Had to work all the time 'cept when I was sick and at night. There was all the time something to do—tend to the young'uns, cook, clean up, wash, iron, my goodness! The tobacco wasn't 'lotted out then, you could tend as much as you thought you could tend, and so we did. We worked hard through the summer saving tobacco time, it was real hard on us. Six weeks saving tobacco.

It's better now, because I ain't got nothing to worry 'bout but myself. Well, I do worry 'bout my children what's living. But thank God they are all healthy and still living. I don't have nobody to fuss with now. And I'm by myself and do just like I want to, sit down if I want to, get up if I want to, wash dishes, make the bed, sweep the floors.

I wouldn't go live with my son or anyone if I got sick, because they have too much racket, too many young'uns. I cain't stand it; I'm nervous. I'd go to the hospital or else go to the rest home. I ain't going to live with my children. Absolutely right, it would be more comfortable for me in a rest home.

I get lonely sometimes, but I just have to sit here and think it out or go to doing something else. I have neighbors but they don't stay long when they come. My sister that lives not too far away spends every night with me. She cooks breakfast and I cook the rest of the meals. Sometimes I cook potatoes and blackeye peas and corn and butterbeans. You know, groceries is so high, I'm telling you the truth when you pay the milkman then go buy your groceries, you just ain't got money enough to do it. I get $157.70 a month [SSI] and that's not enough for me to go on; I have to go on credit sometimes. The children don't help me with money but they help me with vegetables out of their gardens.

It's different, the way people live today, I mean it is. It's worse, worse. Goodness knows, when I got old enough so I could remember, you didn't hear about this killing and all this mess going on now and all this rioting, robbing, pocketbooks snatched, and all this other stuff. The young generation now that's coming up, like my grandchildren in the teens and early twenties, you cain't tell them anything like you could talk to a child way back then and he'd understand. They got a mind of their own and looks like they going to have it that way or that's it. I say you might as well stand up against a rock wall trying to tear it down with a hammer. That's the truth. I have talked to a lot of them and they just won't listen to me. They says, "You just want the world back like it was when you was a child growing up," and I says, "I'll tell you one thing, if it was now like it was then, when I was a child growing up, things would be a hundred times better off." Because people was nearer to God and more people went to church and they didn't have all this recreation, movies and television and all such mess, and I'm telling you the truth, it was wonderful back then. It's not a good world anymore.

Now this doesn't make me afraid to be alone. You see, I just feel like nobody is not going to harm me, because I ain't got no harm against nobody and I feel like they ain't got no harm against me. Although somebody could come and kill me, but if they do, that's the way for you to go. But I just cain't stand it at night alone. I reckon it's because I've been through so much. There went three of my family in a hurry: my husband, and my brother, and my son, in a year, and you talking 'bout heartache and sorrow and trouble, but I really seen it. I'm telling you the truth, I was really loaded up with trouble and sorrow, but thank God I'm getting over it now.

I went to see my dentist and I was telling him I stayed all nervous after my husband died and didn't get over that 'fore my brother died, and then my son died and it was just 'bout to get me. He says, "Well, Mrs. Daniels, I don't know nothing much 'bout the stomach, 'bout the human body; all I knows 'bout is teeth." I says, "I realize that, doctor, but I just want to tell you how nervous I am on the inside, I cain't hardly stand it." He says, "Well, what do you drink for breakfast?" I says, "Coffee." He says, "Well, you stop drinking coffee. What do you drink between meals?" I says, "Orange juice." He says, "Well, you stop drinking orange juice. You take you some Maalox and some Digel and see if that won't help you, and you drink milk for breakfast instead of drinking coffee and orange juice and maybe you'll get better." So I quit coffee and orange juice, I drink grapefruit juice, and it took three months but thank God, I'm so glad I don't have the nervousness now.

What would make life easier? You see those broken brick out there in the yard? I have to be very careful when I go out there. I fell off the porch one time and hurt my arm so bad—ain't they the awfulest steps? I'll tell you one thing, the milkman won't even come up those steps, he always come around to the kitchen. And see, some of the end of the porch is rotting out and the landlord, he was going to fix that too, but he hasn't. You know he don't pick up the rent every month. Sometimes I have 'bout four months' rent for him when he comes because they know the rent will be here and they know I'm true to them with the rent and so they're not going to worry 'bout it. And so when I told him again 'bout the steps and the porch and I told him 'bout what you says, that you thought it was terrible for me to be in here in the condition I was in and the steps like that, he says, "Well, I'll see you one day next week." That week haven't come yet, and that's been well over a month ago.

And if I could have just one thing to make life easier I'd say a bathroom, but I know I won't get none in this house because they going to tear it down. That would be the thing. You see, I got all the junk I want, the furniture, I call it junk. I got all I want now because the more I have the more I have to clean up, and the less I have the less I have to clean.

Elsie West · 67 · "I done worked in a nursing home. I don't care nothing about 'em 'cause they are sort of ill to the people in there."

Mrs. West is a tall, big-boned woman with heavy arms and thighs, her body spilling over tight slacks. Her hair was rolled tight in curlers, and even though we sat indoors throughout the interview, she wore sunglasses. A smile often crinkled her square black face.

She lives at the end of a secondary dirt road in a small trailer which is crowded with furniture. A screened porch has been added to the trailer; in front of the porch are a large number of flowering potted plants.

If I was sick, if it was a long illness, I'd go to the county home, you know the old folk's home, if the children didn't take care of me. All of 'em is working.

I just tell you the truth, I don't like none of the nursing homes, but if something was to happen to me I would have to go to one. I done worked in a nursing home. I don't care nothing about 'em 'cause they are sort of ill to the people in there. They don't treat you as good as they think they do; they scold you and spank you too. Some of the patients was real ill. I was a maid there and some patients would get mad just 'cause I would be dusting around 'em, and 'cause they couldn't do nothing else they'd throw something at me. I guess they needed shaking a little bit, but I don't like to see the staff do that to people like that.

They'd get the patients up sometimes and sit them in chairs, and some of them they had to strap in the chair, but most of the patients laid down all the time. I have been by 'em and they'd ask me to take 'em up, but you see that warn't my job. One, she begged me so hard to

116

stay with her at home so she could go home. I ask her did she have any children and she say yes but they didn't have time to see her. She didn't really need to be in a nursing home; somebody had to be with her 'cause she couldn't control one of her hands. She had just as much sense as I did. A lot of them could've stayed at home if they had someone to come in and clean the house, and be with 'em.

I've never thought of living in with somebody myself. When I get to that place maybe I will, but I want to keep house as long as I can 'cause I don't want to feel like I'm in somebody else's way. I ain't got but two daughters. I feel like if I got so I couldn't help myself one of my daughters would be the onlyest one that could take me—the one that got messed up in the wreck. She is handicapped but she can do in her house. I know my children love me 'cause they show me that they love me, but as long as I can put my foot on a chair and shove it across this house here, I'd rather live here. I got burned out last Christmas and I had to stay away from here a week 'fore I could get back in my house. I just worried myself to death 'bout getting back in this shack.

But so many things is happening these days, I feel like it would be good if I just had a twelve-year-old child here with me—you know the old ones cain't get along too well together. My brother died night 'fore last and they just found him last night—he was living by hisself. Last night now, just 'fore I heard that my brother was dead, a lady come from across the street and told me to close my doors good 'cause there was a man going through there wrapped up in a sheet.

If I didn't have a telephone I couldn't stay here by myself. I feel like if something happen to me the Lord will able me to call somebody.

Eva Jackson · 66 · "I reckon understanding would be one thing to keep people from going to nursing homes. Young people think that they never going to get old."

Mrs. Jackson is short, compact and a little overweight. Her fair-complexioned, round face greets us with a broad smile which conveys warmth and friendliness. A widow for nine years, she shares a house, which belonged to her grandmother, with her son and his family. Her daughter-in-law works in town every day, so Mrs. Jackson does all the family washing and cooking. The land on which the house is situated was originally farmland worked by her husband until he went into "public work." Now it produces only enough to provide the family with vegetables.

Mrs. Jackson fell and broke her arm a year ago and several years before that had a broken leg. Her independent spirit and favorable living conditions—a house shared with her son and his family, a brother's family nearby—made it possible for her to avoid hospitalization. On both occasions, as soon as she was able to be up and around, she was back at her gardening and housekeeping.

Every year, the first Sunday in August, we have a community picnic. We have been doing this for about fifty-five years, I reckon. Christmas we'll have our Christmas tree. And then our women society, we have a supper and invite our husbands and boyfriends to the supper. We just have one society—United Methodist Women. We have a program every first Tuesday night—it's on the Bible, and we talk about people in the community that needs anything, we go to rest homes and visit, just things like that.

But sometimes you get blue—everybody gets lonesome. I still miss my husband. I miss doing things together. Like he would tell me to fix what I had to eat and we would ride out and find a table and eat together—something like a picnic. After we ate we would ride around some more and maybe visit a sick person that we knew. I have heard people say they wished they had never married, but I've never regretted the day I was married. So somedays I am blue and lonely, but it's all right. It's about as good as could be expected.

I have a lot of friends. You don't know what your friends mean to you till you don't have them. This girl I spent the night with last Saturday night was my cousin; we was raised together. She seems more like a sister to me than anything else. It's not many days that we don't call each other.

A telephone's a good thing for old people. I think just as much of that telephone as a old woman does a dip of snuff. I get lonesome sometimes and I get around here and call up somebody and talk. Yes I do. I think every old person should have a telephone—just for emergency if nothing else.

And I think everybody should have running water when they get old. You take anybody old and have to draw water, it's just bad on them. And then I think they should have a bathroom, 'cause I'm telling you now, you take an older person having to get out in the cold to the outside is just rough. I'd hate to be without either one.

It's been a year this past November, I broke my arm—doctor said I just crushed it all to pieces. I told him I got drunk and fell in a rock pile! Really, I was out there working on the yard; I was on my knees a pulling a little old honeysuckle vine and I reckon my hand slipped, I don't know. The next thing I know I was laying over in a rock pile, great big rocks. I just laid right over in that and crushed my wrist nearly all to pieces.

I done managed myself. I think back now, I don't know how I managed. I've had my leg broke too and I went along and picked beans on a crutch. I'd lean over on my crutch and reach over and pick beans with my leg broke, and with my arm broke I done my cooking and everything. I made up my bread and all with that little fork. I'd take one hand and get it fixed and I'd make my biscuits there. I just don't like loaf bread; I bet I don't buy a loaf of bread a year. Of course it wasn't decent-looking biscuits, but they were all right. You know, when you're bound to have to do a thing, you can do it. When bound comes around, you can do a lot of things. It's do or starve, so you do.

I didn't want to go to a hospital or to a rest home when I got hurt. Maybe rest homes are all right; you hear somebody say they are the best things in the world and then the next person that comes up makes you think about the best thing to do is strike a match to them and burn them down. I don't know whether I would want to go to a rest home or not. I might have to. Now this friend of mine, she's colored, and she lives over there in Mill Town; she's in Mount Pleasant Rest Home. She was sitting up in a wheelchair when I got there one day and wanted to lay back down again. So this colored girl that works there comes in and just put her in that bed any old way. She never ask her if she was laying all right; she didn't get her comfortable at all, just throwed her up in the bed and didn't try to fix her at all, and she walked out. All they're looking for is five-thirty and payday; they just do enough to get by with and go.

Some people don't think about what old people need. I reckon understanding would be one thing to keep people from going to nursing homes, 'cause a lot of young people think that they never going to get old; they think they are going to stay young always. Maybe old people need a little more sympathy and understanding, a little more respect. Some people think when you get old you don't need to go nowhere—you done been all you should go—all you need to do is set at home and not do nothing.

Mabel Jones · 72 · "I wouldn't have the money to pay to go to a rest home. I wouldn't have the money to pay somebody to stay with me either."

Mrs. Jones, her face pale, her brow creased in anxiety, and her body sagging, sat dejectedly throughout the interview. She is seldom to be found at home in her small box-like, green, cement-block house for she is afraid to be alone at night and supports herself by helping out sick neighbors.

I've been down and not feeling good for the last month. My arthritis been real bad. I haven't been to church in several Sundays for I ain't been able. I see my neighbors, they don't visit much but they real good about carrying me to church. I don't hardly ever ask anybody to carry me anywhere 'less I think they are really going. They've got their own work to do. People have better conveniences, like electricity and all, these days but in the old days they had more time. They'd go to see their neighbors. Course we're living in a time now we don't know what's best for our ownselves, never mind to know what'd help somebody else.

There are so many sick people who need somebody to help 'em. I lost my husband when my baby was small, so I had to stay with people to make support for her and myself. I worked as long as I could, but with my nerves and headaches I don't think I could work in that strong a job now. What I do is go around, help people who's sick, or do housework or something like that. That's all I'm able to do. I didn't work regular last year; I just go over and stay with somebody maybe a week and somebody else, maybe a day or two, something like that.

When I was able to work I enjoyed it. Now I feel so bad I don't enjoy myself. I been going downhill for the last two years. But I reckon you got a lot to be thankful for if you can get around at all. I reckon it's a good thing just to be alive—so many things happen when you alive—there ain't no good things happen when you dead.

I ain't got no business staying alone, my health so bad. Well, anybody been used to being around somebody, then they start living by their-selves, it's lonesome for them. Now I don't mind in the daytime by myself, but at night I don't like it. At night I just don't like to be here too much by myself. Most times I go somewhere at night to stay with a friend. It's a job, though, to have to go somewhere every night. I mean you're going to have to get up and go the next day, get up and come back home. Course I most always loved home; I like to stay at home all the time. Don't like to all the time be running around.

I just don't know what I'd do if I couldn't care for myself. I won't worry about that till it gets here. I think rest homes help people. But I wouldn't have the money to pay to go to a rest home. I wouldn't have the money to pay somebody to come stay with me either. I just don't know. I believe I'd rather stay in my own home as long as I could.

displaced

"They really do nothing all day."

Irma Bunn · Nursing Home Aide · "I enjoy old folks so much, if I had the money I would work at the nursing home for free, I really would."

Irma Bunn, a middle-aged, thickset, black woman of fifty is a smiling, motherly person who has been working as an aide in a nursing home for five years.

I've been working in Pleasant Hill Nursing Home five years till today. My position is nurse's aide and I work night shift. I check all my patients to see is everybody OK. They're checked every two hours. Some patients have to be checked on even more often because of their condition. There is some patients that can talk; I ask if there's anything they'd like to have before the next check time. We check for wetness in patients. We also make sure that everybody is in bed because sometimes we have patients who may wander.

There are about two hundred people in the nursing home altogether. Each aide looks after fifty patients at night because there are four aides and two hundred patients. Each aide usually looks after at least ten to twelve patients that need total care, but sometimes we are short staffed and we look after fifteen. We only have four aides on the eleven-to-seven shift at night for each side—there are two sides. But like I said, most times we are short staffed and usually there's only two for each side. We really have time only to care for the sickest patients. Total care means turning them every two hours, taking care of bedsores, making sure their heads are turned the right way when they're given tube feedings. When we turn them we have to make sure that the tubes are straight and curved to the back of the pillow. But some patients can look after themselves; they can go to the bathroom themselves, or they can turn over in bed themselves. The rest of the patients need some care, but not as much. They will ring bells when they want water, when they want to eat snacks between meals, or something like that. When we see the light then we go and see what they want. We look in on everybody every two hours.

Some of the patients do help the other patients. We have several patients who can get up out of bed and they will carry water to other patients. Sometimes they will get up and ring the bell for other patients.

I know it's not enough aides. I think there should be six aides to each side. I think we could use twelve aides good and then everybody could do what they should do, have time to do it, and do it the right way. Now, only the most serious cases are done properly. You do the major things that has to be done. Some little things like mouth care and things that can go undone usually are left undone because you don't have time. The reason is some patients' rooms you go in and you can do everything you need to do maybe in twenty minutes, and the next room it may take the patient twenty minutes to get him in a notion to do what it is he needs to do.

Most of the aides are young people. They want a job, they come in and talk to the supervisor. After she hires them, they get five days orientation, which I don't think is enough. They only learn to make a bed, they are told how to clean bedpans and how to turn patients, and they are also told how to do vital signs. But some of the aides can't grasp that in five days. Because as you know when you take blood pressure, a temp, or respiration, your memory kind of runs with your hands, you gotta keep it in mind what the number was and write it all down at the same time. Two or three months after they are hired, they'll come back and say I still don't know how to take a pressure. They have a nurse to come out and train them to do the vital signs, do the beds, and how to turn a patient. But after the five days, they are on the hall with another aide who has been working longer.

When the nursing home runs short of aides, some aides with no experience are hired—nobody has even been sick in their own home but they say they can do the job. When they come in the supervisor will give them just a few hours training, then let the new aide work on the floor with another aide. I think the aides like the kind of work they do, but because they don't think they get enough money, it makes them not stay on the job.

But as far as the patients, I think they really fall in love with the patients. I really think it applies to all the aides. Because most of the aides I've worked with so far, they get really close to the old people. You never pick your patients, but there are some patients you get close enough to they feel just like family. It's just like a parent to you. Because some of them don't have visitors. Some have children who never come to see them, then we have others somebody comes every day to visit them. The reason the aides can get so close to the patients is that often the patient will see you as somebody they know. They will call you by their daughter's name or some sister's name or some friend they have.

I think the most difficult patients are the cancer patients, because they are very hard to please. You can do all you can and it seems like they feel you're working against them. I don't know the reason for that. I have asked patients and I have asked the nurses and it's no answer. They are the most unhappy, especially the men. The women get use to it quicker. The men most times they will tell you, "I use to work and now I cain't work, and it seems like you all don't want me to do what I can do," but usually it's nothing that they can do. If you go to give them a drink of water, they cain't hold the glass without pouring the water on themselves. They say they can walk, but when you help them get up you find out they cain't. And it runs mostly with men to be more difficult to deal with than women.

The aides I've worked with, so far, have not been nasty to the patients. I have heard aides say on the outside, "The patient got so rotten with me, I could have just spanked them." But I've never seen that done.

Yes, it's true that sometimes the floors are dirty. Sometimes the patient gets up and starts to the bathroom and before they can make it, the urine is coming, and they cain't help it. Usually they will stop, sometimes they will fall, but most times we've been lucky to catch the patient by the time he falls or by the time he rings his bell. When we get there we make that the first step, to clean it up. If the patient steps in it, she will fall. It's very slick, but I've never had but one patient to get a fracture.

Yes, some patients miss their things but I'm afraid to say that it gets stolen. It does get misplaced. We had one patient who had a nice watch and the watch got gone, and every aide the nurse and supervisor checked everywhere, and we could not find the watch. But there was another patient who just rides around in her wheelchair and picks up milk cartons and paper from a cookie, and she had an old sweater in her drawer rolled up, so we opened it up. And among all this paper and scraps there was the watch. So sometimes we have patients who collect things and they will put them in their drawer, thinking it's theirs, sometimes they don't even know what it is. In some cases, it might be the staff taking things. But the places I've worked, I haven't had nothing to prove that to be true.

Yes, patients are tied to the bed or chair. But that's for a reason. Patients will get up and wander off, and they cain't balance themselves. So when they are put in wheelchairs, they have what they call restraints. They are made like a little apron and it ties—they're slack enough so they can move around in the chair—but still it has to be tied tight enough so they cain't untie it, because if they get up and start walking, they fall. It doesn't apply to most patients, maybe only four or five. There are some restrained in bed, and that's because, when we have tube feedings and sometimes intravenous feedings, they pull the tubings out. And in some cases they have to restrain them in bed because they will get out and crawl out over the rail. We've had that to happen once or twice. They fall and maybe get a small slash on the forehead or their jaw or ear where they fall from their bed.

I don't see much difference in the skilled nursing facility side and the intermediate care facility side because we give good care on both sides. We might have to spend a little more time on one side, but I think it's about the same because everybody is treated the same and the staff is taking as much time as they can with every patient. There's not that much difference in their conditions either, except for some like multiple sclerosis patients, you have to be very careful with them and check very well.

I think there are lots of patients could be at home. We have some patients, if they only had someone to watch them, make sure they stay inside, watch when they walk that they gonna be on a safe spot, they could stay home. They are not at home for different reasons. Mostly, they don't have people to take care of them. If they have children, the children have to work. I think basically they are not at home by the children not being able financially to take care of the parents. If the children had enough money that they could live without working a regular job, they could take care of a lot of the older people at home.

If I could run a nursing home, I would have meetings and ask the families to visit as often as they could. I would have programs to include the older people, the ones who could talk. I would have things like talk shows, workshops, or give them an open opportunity to talk about themselves. If I had four or five cancer patients, four or five stroke patients, or whatever, I would put each of their own together, and let them talk about themselves among each other.

I would hire more people. I would try to have enough on staff to take care of all the patients. I would try to see that each person was paid enough so they would feel like what they were doing is being credited. I think an aide should be trained at least six or eight weeks. Because for one thing, you will forget these things if you don't do them often enough. It's a hard job working as an aide in a nursing home, but if there were enough people on staff, it wouldn't be.

I keep doing the work because I enjoy the patients. The reason I do it at nights is because I work in a funeral home during the day directing funerals, and I never know what's coming up. So I have to work nights. Otherwise I would work three to eleven [pm] because I would get more time to see what the families are like, get time to talk with the patients, and see more of them. Because at night, some of the patients you never learn—you just know their faces and their names. You only know what you read in the chart about them. If you were there in the evening, you'd get a chance to talk with them.

The funeral work, that's a part-time thing. I don't work unless a funeral comes up. That can be three days in a row, sometimes four, and sometimes we can go a whole week with nothing. If I work the night before, I come in and sleep about two hours. Then after the funeral I would come back and go back to bed. Sometimes that's maybe two or maybe three hours sleep.

I have three children at home, but they're grown. I have a grandbaby that's two years old, but his mother takes care of him. My oldest son works with the county; I have a son in school who's seventeen, and there's Mary and the baby. Mary is eighteen and she works at Pleasant Hill now, night shift. I have another daughter who works at Mill Town Hospital from three in the afternoon until twelve at night. She takes care of Mary's baby at night. We do the cooking in our house together. We share. My husband cooks in the morning and me and the girls we exchange days and cook.

My husband, he's a carpenter. He's self employed, and he's a sub-contractor. He keeps up good in the summer time but he gets lost in the winter, because the weather gets bad and he doesn't have anything big to do; he just does little piece jobs on the inside like putting up cabinets, sheet rock, panelling.

I enjoy old folks so much, if I had the money I would work at the nursing home for free, I really would. Because a lot of those old people, I get real close to them. Sometimes I guess I get too close. We had one lady in her nineties. She was the sweetest little lady I most ever met. I don't know why I felt like I did. She had family to visit. She kinda petted me like, and she felt just like my grandmother. I named her Grandma Goldilocks. And that's what I called her till she died. I went back to work and they told me she had passed. It really hurt. When I went down to the funeral home to view the body, I told the undertaker how close I was to her and he asked me to stay for the funeral. I couldn't because I had to go back to work that night, and I had to get some sleep, but I went to the funeral home the next morning about time they opened and stayed about ten minutes and just looked at her. She was real pretty. She looked just like a little doll baby.

My grandmother lived at home with us. My mother took my grandmother in our house when I was about five years old, and she lived with us until I was nineteen. I loved her dearly, and I called her Mama until she died. It could be why I like old people. And then another thing—when I moved into Mill Town all the other young ladies worked and I didn't. There were about five older people lived nearby. I use to do their shopping for them, and they would get their checks and I would go cash them, help them get their groceries, and some of them I helped them pick their clothes. I just had a lot of old friends. My father use to live with me until he had a stroke; he died two years ago. He was in the hospital first, and then the doctor told him that he would need to go to a nursing home. He wasn't there long when he had another stroke and they put him back in the hospital and that's when he passed. If he had got so I could handle him I was going to bring him back home. My son who was at home and my husband could have helped me with his bath and I think I could have managed. But he never got so he could use himself enough to come back home.

The nurses in the nursing home are good. The ones I worked with all these years; I find them all to be good. Like I said we're short staffed and something comes up and both aides are busy, and the nurse will leave the desk and come out and help us. But the head staff, I don't think they clearly understand what really goes on on the wards because they're doing the paper work, and whatever the nurse says is what they have to go by, but just to see it and to know it is different. When they see the patients the morning shift have gotten them up and got their clothes on and everybody looks fine. The head people need to come through some nights and just look at the things that really go on, because they really don't know. They expect you to keep bedpans washed, have wheelchairs clean, do it every night. When aides started talking about how much work there was and how everything couldn't get finished, then they started the plan that on Thursday night we did wheelchairs and on Friday nights we would do bedpans. Wednesday nights we do refrigerators. There's one small refrigerator on each floor, and on Wednesday nights we would clean them, defrost them. Some nights that's easy to do and some nights it's not. Sometimes people put stuff back in, and instead of closing it up somebody might turn over a carton of milk, and don't clean up the spills, and from one thing to the other it can be a real mess.

I don't think that's the right thing to do, to clean up as well as look after the patients, for two reasons. For one reason, I don't see it to be sanitary enough to come out to clean up around a desk, and a patient calls you and you really ain't got the time right then to wash your hands. You got to go put your hands right then right on the wound or catch hold to his face.

But, still, I would rather work in a nursing home. I would rather be moving around, talking to the patients, thinking about what they want, doing different things. Taking any job that means sitting behind a desk, I think I would get bored. Thinking about it from the value side, also, I would rather be in a nursing home. If I'm typing, that work will wait; if I leave my desk full, I know it's gonna be there tomorrow. But if I have patients to take care of, I need to take care of them then because tomorrow somebody else will be doing what I needed to do.

It would be nice to bring old people and young people together in a nursing home. From my point of view when you take four or five old people and four or five young people and four or five children and get together, you would be surprised the things they will talk about. It would be different than if it was two or three older people talking by themselves. I take neighbors, older people, out and eat with them, and a lot of times I take them to the park. I carry a few down in the country and we go fishing, and usually they will call me back and ask me when I'm going again.

I think it's great to mix the ages because you learn a lot from the old people and they learn a lot from you. Take when my children were small. I learned a lot from old people. You just don't think every time when something happens to a kid what to do. And some older person might come along and tell you some little home remedy and it works. My grandmother, she partly raised me, because my mother worked two days a week. My grandmother was able then to do the cooking. She taught me how to cook, and she would wash—at that time they were washing from a tub, a wash board, and this big pot on the outside. We had a well in our back yard that had a tin bucket and when you drawed the water up you had to pour it in another bucket to take it where you had to go. I had fun with my grandmother. She taught me how to make homemade soap. She taught me sewing, with my hands first, then how to sew on the sewing machine.

My grandmother use to read the Bible, and the newspaper. She would tell me to always read the headlines first, that's about the biggest thing in the paper. She was very hard about having respect for other people. She always told me regardless of what I heard or what somebody said, to be mannerable. If someone said something that I thought wasn't right, not to say that it wasn't right. Then, later if I wanted, to go back to the person and ask them why did they say it in that way, that I felt like it was wrong. She always taught me to respect older people and if I went someplace, make sure that I said thank you when I get off the car. If someone gave me something like a stick of gum, to make sure I said thank you. And wherever I eat, if the people said a blessing or didn't, for me always to whisper a little prayer.

Betty Morrison · Family Care Home Owner · "They really do nothing all day."

Mrs. Morrison, black, plump, graying and sixty-three years old, boards five women in three bedrooms of her home. The green frame house is single-story, and has a narrow open porch fronting a small garden crowded with trees and shrubbery. The house is also crowded with furniture, family photographs and knick-knacks.

Mrs. Morrison smiled often and appeared to have a warm, cordial relationship with the people she cared for. On our second visit we observed one of the boarders, a blind woman on crutches, with deformities of her legs caused by burns, being given verbal directions to the bathroom. One resident was still asleep, one sat in the kitchen. There were two vacancies in the home at that time. The woman we had hoped to see again, a former resident of Ashton, had been admitted to a hospital with heart failure soon after our first visit, and had died in a nursing home.

I used to be in restaurant service, in cafe work, and domestic work; then all my children got grown and left me here by myself. I said I ain't going to stay. My sister-in-law was keeping old people in her home and she said, "Why don't you get some people?" And I said, "Well, I think I will try." And guess what, everything worked out okay. So that's how I got started. And I just enjoys it. I do everything myself, but sometimes my daughter will come and stay or Sister Harris down the street, she will stay like when I go to pay my bills. Sometimes I go fishing. I tell my daughter, "Look here, I want to go to the water." She'll say, "Mama, I get off at one o'clock." And I say, "Okay, then I will go after one o'clock." And she come out here later.

They ain't no trouble, nobody. They are just as humble as babies. They get up and wash up in the morning and put their clothes on. Call them to breakfast, they eat. My lord, they eat like mens! They tell me I give them too much, but I rather for them to come to the table and leave full than to come hungry and go away hungry. They won't go out on the porch till after the spirituals come on at noon.

They can do some things on their own. Most of the time I help Miss Lena with her bath, sometimes I have to help her walk—when she get up she stumbles. There is another lady on crutches, another who walks with a walker, but she is doing a little better and I'm trying to make her put her walker down. They really do nothing all day. Lena look at papers and things, she love to look at papers. Miss Gladys look at a book once in a while, but Miss Mae, she is partially blind, and they told me at the hospital that there was nothing else they could do for her. They just look at T.V. or listen to the radio. There are missionary people that come by sometimes and have prayer on Sunday. Visitors, that's what they need. Somebody to cheer them up from their families. Some come more often than others. But Miss Lena's niece, Emily, comes sometimes once in two months, sometimes she comes once in three months. Miss Moore, her niece comes and get her. They got her Friday and just brought her back yesterday afternoon, and they takes her to church. So Lena said she was going to go to church too, and I told Emily to get her some rubber panties, I said I think they cost $11, and I will take her to church. She cain't hold her water, and I couldn't take her spilling the water like that.

See, they're all Medicaid patients. Medicaid pays $322 a month; they get $17.80 for spending on clothes and personal things. But the family takes that. So I said, "Well, you all are getting it, but since they are here with me I know more what they need." I said, "When the money comes I'm going to spend some on what they need, and then I'm going to take what I done spent out of the $17.80." Whenever Lena's niece takes the money, she says she's going to bring her fruit. She don't never say nothing about bringing her clothes. I tell their families that when I carry them out I want them to look neat. I want my people to look nice when I take them out. I told Lena's niece that she needs some shoes. She brought her them little shoes to slip her foot in. I said to Lena, "Well, she still ain't bought you nothing to go out with to carry you to the clinic. You got to go to the clinic with bedroom shoes all the time." Then her niece brought her a pair of her own shoes but they were too large. She was walking with a klunka-klunka-klunka-klunk. So I just go on and give it to them myself. I feel like one day I will get mine.

I don't know—I just don't know. I tells them when their peoples put them here, "Don't feel bad. Them young folks ain't got time for old peoples now. That's why I wouldn't mistreat you no better I would my mama." 'Cause I'm getting old too and I don't know, my kids may mistreat me and I may have to go somewhere one day.

Lena Wilson · "70 or 80" · "I'd like to get out, do a little work, make me a little change—ain't nothing like making your own change.

At the time of our first visit, Miss Wilson, a black woman, was a resident in the home of Mrs. Morrison. A pleasant, friendly woman, she is short and stout, with round plump face and white hair. Well liked by Mrs. Morrison and all the residents of the home, she is affectionately nicknamed "Shorty."

Never married, she lived in her sister Mary's Ashton home until Mary sold the house and they rented another in Mill Town. Soon thereafter, Mary died and Miss Wilson, herself unwell, was unable to pay the rent. Her sister's daughter then placed her in the Morrison Rest Home. Miss Wilson, who gives her age as seventy or eighty (her niece says she is 85), spends a good deal of her time thinking about the past and reminiscing about her long years in service with a family whose children she helped raise but whom she has not seen for many years.

Oh, I've been here a good while, ever since my sister died—Mary. Well, I don't know exact time, but been a good little bit. No Ma'am, I never married. I seen nobody I wanted to latch onto. It kind o' looked like the menfolk so sorry—want you to work for them 'stead of them working for you. There's seven of us and all of 'em married but me. I'm a twin, and he [my twin brother] married two or three times. I'm the last pea in the dish. Yeah, I'm the last one. All of 'em gone to glory but me. I stayed there in the house by myself a while after my sister died, but wasn't nobody there but me and I couldn't keep up the house by myself. My feet and legs was swelled. Emily, that's Mary's daughter, my niece, she's the one looks after me—mighty nice to me, mighty nice. Oh, I has some other nieces and nephews, but they're all up North. They don't know no more 'bout me, looking after me, than they looking after you, and I'll tell you what's the truth, I hardly ever hear from 'em. Emily's the only one I have down here. She makes it here to see me every month—once a month, sometimes oftener than that.

I'm not lonely. I done got use to it. I'm just as happy by myself as I had a house full. T'ain't none in my way. It's better to be by yourself. 'Cause you have folks, they'll mess up your things or take your things or something like that, you know. 'Course, these folks is mighty nice to me and all, and I try to be nice to them like they are to me. I've got no room to grumble. If I could have whatever I want—in the eating line—I'd like some canned goods. But if I had just one wish, it would be for plenty money. I'd save it and live off of it. That's what I'd do. I wouldn't move from here, not unless there was cause. But I'd get me some clothes, then I'd try to get me a little canned goods, you know. Save that for hard times. I'd like to be doing something, if I could.

I use to wash and iron for Mrs. Hunt. I went there and looked after them children—oh, a long time till they got grown. The children was just little tots running around. I think the old people, the mother and father's dead. There was four girls. I don't know any of them's dead or not. Before I moved out here, when I's living in Ashton, they'd come. Yes, they was mighty nice for coming to see me. Mr. Hunt was a railroad man; he had to go wherever they sent him. And so they'd send him backwards and forwards, come back home, then they'd send him away to Raleigh. I'd go down there too and Mary and I worked for her here too. I stayed right there and looked after the children.

Well, now I just sit around here. Yes'm, I sit around. I just sit here and read a book and sometimes do a little hand sewing. I've got a little television of my own here. I don't like to mess with other folks' things, 'cause they'd get wrong with me and I wouldn't be able to pay for it. I'd like to get out and kind o' do a little work, you know. Like a little cleaning in the house or washing dishes and all. Yes, Ma'am. I'd like to make me a little change—ain't nothing like making your own change.

Ethel Black · 80 · "Companionship. I think that does people more good than most anything else."

Mrs. Black's pale, wan face expressed sadness and some apprehension. Her gray hair was neatly combed, her compact, stocky figure comfortably clad in a cotton, print dress. She seemed somewhat guarded in her description of life in the rest home saying, "I wish I could tell you just how it all is."

A new, brick, single-story house, Laurel Rest Home had its full complement of five occupants. The rest home is one of three owned by a couple who lived nearby. Each home was in the charge of a house-keeper who attended to the daily routine and care of the home and residents. Laurel Rest Home, situated in a lower to middle class neighborhood, was far superior in structure and furnishings to the home of Mrs. Morrison but lacked the atmosphere of warmth and empathy which Mrs. Morrison, herself, gave to her home.

We used to live in Mill Town all the time. I have a daughter here in Ashton and I have three sons, but everyone of them three live a long way. The daughter's the only real close relative I have here.

I'm not well. I had two severe heart arrests and I was a week or two in a hospital for that. And then, six months after I left the hospital, we got a notice from the hospital that they had found cancer. The slip [hospital record] had been lost and they had just found it again somehow. Well, there I'd been six months wearing cancer—didn't know what it was going to do. It kind of upset our whole family.

And so then I had an operation for that—for cancer of the uterus. And then I had phlebitis in my left leg and it got up to my hip and it went up to my stomach. My blood was clotted and I stayed in the hospital a month or more with that. I never have been able to do anything since, not work or take care of myself. I did take care of myself before all this and was able to do anything and go any place I pleased. In the meantime, after I had my heart seizures, about a month or two later, my husband died in a rest home up here. The reason he was up here is so my daughter could help me look after him and all, and he died and they had put me in the same rest home he was in after my operation, so I was in that same rest home where he died. And when I got able, of course, I went back to my daughter's. And then last year I had a terrible pain in my foot and I just thought it'd kill me. I had to go to the hospital for that and I had to stay twenty-eight days. After that, I wasn't able to walk until gradually I got a little better, and now I walk with a cane.

I came here to the Laurel Rest Home because my daughter couldn't look after me because she works, and I couldn't look after myself. I had no place to go from the hospital, and she tried to get me in a nursing home and they wouldn't take me there because I could walk with a walker and a cane. Of course, I gradually got better, but she still had no place for me because she had to work. It was either me in a home or quit her job. She tried everything she could and they were helping her; the lady at the hospital, and the doctor, they were trying to place me someplace. But I wasn't able to look after myself. I'm not able to look after myself now. I'm eighty years old. And at last they put me here, and I've been here about a year.

The woman that runs the home takes care of everybody here that's able to look after their own selves as far as their personal attendance goes. You know, like washing and feeding yourself and going to the bathroom. She doesn't do those things for any of them.

She does all the cleaning and cooking, everything like that. We make our beds, and she vacuums the floors and we can dust the room. As far as the home goes, I couldn't ask to be in a better place for somebody like myself. But it is depressing staying here.

We have one lady, Mrs. Mangum, she cain't talk, her tongue's paralyzed. If you're used to her, you can understand her some, but she's in her seventies, seventy-seven or something like that. And Mrs. Anderson is ninety-one and I often tell them, "Aw, she's got more sense than all the rest of us put together." But I can tell Mrs. Anderson's failing, because she's getting to where she just cain't eat hardly. I feel like she needs something a little special fixed for her which she doesn't get. She says she just cain't eat that food to save her life, says she just forces it down. We don't have too big a variety in our food. The same thing, same thing, right over and over.

It's not that bigger homes are better than smaller ones. No, it's just according to who's in it. Yeah, it all starts right there—companionship. I think that does people more good than most anything else. Just having someone else to talk to. I wish I could tell you just how it all is, but I couldn't do that. Besides Mrs. Anderson and Mrs. Mangum, we have Mrs. Hill; she has a broken hip and stays in her room most of the time. Then there's Mrs. Riggsbee in the room next to me, we used to be friends a long, long time ago, but her mind's not so good now.

It is lonely. Not as lonely as it could be, I don't reckon, but it would be to anybody that wanted to stir around and mingle with people. Because when I first came here nobody ever said, "Good Morning," never in the world. I was tired of telling them, "Good Morning," I'd never been used to doing like that, you know. I'm used to people being jolly. But now they all speak. Two ladies did come one night, wanted to fix for us to have games and things like that, but the people here won't play games. Mrs. Anderson sits there and she cain't hear a sound; she plays solitary all day or puts puzzles together. And Mrs. Hill don't do a thing in the world, or Mrs. Mangum, either one of 'em. Mrs. Hill cain't see very well—she doesn't even read the newspaper. But Mrs. Rigsbee does, she's as sweet as she can be. She gets things tangled up, she cain't remember. Well, no need of me saying that, I cain't remember either.

My daughter comes by most anytime if I need anything at all, and then some weekends she takes me out to her place. I stay here most of the time because she has a husband and a little girl and I think, maybe, they want to be getting out and doing something. That's the only holiday they have is on the weekend. But I do go to church just about every Sunday when I'm here. I don't get to go to our Baptist Church. Of course, I think that's all the church there is, but the Salvation Army people come by and get Mrs. Anderson every Sunday and she invited me to go with her, and I've been going with her down there to her church now for a good little while and I really enjoy it. When I feel like it, I do a little sewing, mend up my clothes. Sometimes I have dresses that's too short or too long or what have you, or too small, too large or something, and I do little stuff like that. I cain't do much. You see, I have arthritis so bad in my hands. If I could wish for anything I want, it would be for health, so I could take care of myself. But, you see, since my husband's dead, I don't know where I'd stay.

Ethel Black's Daughter · "What is my mother to do, die?"

During the interview with Mrs. Black in Laurel Rest Home, her daughter came to visit and participated freely in the interview. She was very upset at having had to place her mother in a family care home and spoke bitterly about the attitude of physicians towards Medicaid patients and the lack of professional and community services.

When mother went on Medicaid, I called every doctor in Mill Town. Well, would you believe it, I took the yellow pages, and not one doctor would take her. I was cussed, I was talked ugly to. "We can't take a Medicaid because we don't get our money—Social Services don't pay us; we have to have our money." I begged. I said, "What is my mother to do, die?" "Oh, take her to the clinic." I said, "She doesn't need to be there. She needs a private physician. What am I to do?" The doctor's receptionist said, "Oh, I don't know. You'll find a way." This is what hurts, the way I was talked to by the receptionists. I would explain to them, "I'm not a millionaire. I have my family. I can't afford to pay expenses for my family plus my mother."

One time, Mother was in the hospital with cancer and my little girl was in the hospital the same day. They both had surgery. Got my little girl home and bam, my husband had a heart attack. He was in intensive care. What could I do? My hands were tied.

And then, that was the talk that I got when I tried to get a doctor for mother. Knowing that my time, too, was valuable, rather than having to sit with her all day in a clinic. She needed to go to a doctor that would take her. But no doctor would touch her whatsoever, and she needed medical attention. Finally, through the goodness of his heart, Dr. M was the only one in Mill Town that would take her. And then, Dr. W, who is in neurology, saw her for her high blood pressure. And he and Dr. W treated her just the same as if she had been a millionaire.

After mother left the hospital, I tried desperately to get someone to come to my home and take care of her. I offered $75 a week for somebody to work from nine o'clock in the morning until four in the afternoon. All they'd have to do five days a week was prepare her breakfast, stay and fix her some lunch. Now I don't mean a great big, heavy meal, I mean open a can of soup, fix a sandwich or something, then stay till an hour before I got home. That would only leave her home an hour alone, and then, too, my little girl would be in from school by that time. We thought we were offering a very good salary, but it was impossible to get anyone! They said, "Why should I do it? I can draw more unemployment. I can get more from the welfare." This was the answer I got. I had no choice but to put her in this home.

What we need is stiffer laws that would make people accept jobs, rather than to draw unemployment and welfare, where they are qualified and capable to accept these jobs. The social services department, God bless them, they helped me every way they could to find somebody. One woman told me, and I'll tell you her exact words, "I'm not working for that salary. If you can get more [from social service] "I'll take the job, but they're going to have to pay me more." And she was telling me what to do before I ever hung up. I fired her before I could hire her!

Mattie Nichols · Owner of Restful Place · "I always wanted to be a nurse but I didn't get to do that; so this is the next best thing."

Mrs. Nichols is the proud owner of a home for the aged and infirm which she and her husband recently built with a minimum of professional help.

The home is a single-story, long, red brick building with a small,

*cement front porch leading to grounds that are bare except for a few
shrubs.*

*Nineteen people can be accommodated, eighteen in double occu-
pancy rooms and one in a single room. The bedrooms, leading off a
wide corridor, are adequately but impersonally furnished with stan-
dardized furniture. No pictures, photographs, flowers or personal
knick-knacks are in evidence. A dayroom has chairs for residents
ranged against two walls; a large television set is the focal point of the
room. The dayroom leads into a dining room with several small tables
and this room, in turn, leads into a large and modern kitchen, with
many shining stainless steel fixtures. Floors throughout the home are
covered with vinyl and, in general, the pervading atmosphere is that of
a small hospital. The home is orderly, scrupulously clean, but un-
homelike.*

*What appears to be lacking are any organized recreational or social
activities, and there are no religious services for the residents, mostly
black, who, seemingly, spend their days in idleness and boredom.*

*Mrs. Nichols, a black woman in her fifties, is tall and well built. An
extremely friendly woman who smiles often, she seems to genuinely
care about the welfare of her charges, to do all she can for them and to
be content with the way she has chosen to make her living.*

I didn't have any special training, but I have always liked people. I
always wanted to be a nurse but I didn't get to do that, so I said well,
since I got this old, this is the next best thing. There is a lot to do to get
a home built, I tell you. But we finally managed to do it, and we've been
in here a year. I hope some day that we can pay off everything. I worked
very hard. I worked out here with the men; we mostly built this
ourselves. Of course, you know, we had to get somebody to do our
plumbing and had to have an electrician, and we had a very nice brick
mason, but I worked out here with him. I drove the tractor, hauled
block, made mortar, painted, and I bought all the furnishing for the
inside. In fact, I looked after the whole thing myself.

I like it fine; I am here almost twenty-four hours a day. The state
requires us to have four people to help. I have two ladies that work in
the daytime who come on about seven or eight in the morning till
three, and then two ladies who come on at three and stay till eleven. Of
course I am here all the time, and I have a lady that comes in at eleven
at night and works till seven next morning. My husband, he's here, and
my daughter, she's here some. She is a teacher in Virginia and she help

during the summer and sometimes comes here on holidays.

I can accommodate nineteen. Right now I just have one vacancy, that's all. Most of the residents are able to get around by themselves. I have two or three here that come from nursing homes. Now most of them, the Department of Social Service places them. That's because they don't have anybody at home to take care of them, and they need to be cared for. Here we cook for them, wash, iron, give them medication or whatever needs to be done. The baths, we do that ourselves to be sure that it is properly done. We don't give any injections, all medications is by mouth. I carry them to the doctor or hospital if they need to go. Wherever they need to go to, that's where I carry them.

I usually carry them to the beauty parlor, at least once a month, and then they have to get their medicine. They get the Medicaid stickers to pay for their medicines, but they have to have an extra fifty cents for each bottle over the stickers. Jinny Young has about five or six bottles to be filled. And some of the bottles or some of the medications will last a month, and then some don't last that long. Sometimes they have to have some of the bottles filled twice a month. Different little things they have to have, so they don't have much money left over after that. See, they are mostly Medicaid patients, and social services just allow them $17.70 a month for anything personal they have to have, clothes and all.

There had been some young ladies coming in once a week to play games and make different things, but for the last two or three weeks they haven't been here. They had some kind of hold up on account of money. Miss Andrews from social services brought them down here on their first trip. They haven't been back, but anyway, we got crayons and a ball. The bus used to pick the residents up, the senior citizens' bus, and carry them to the Recreation Center on Center Street. They had that for a good while, but they don't anymore. I don't know why. I guess they are out of funds. So the ladies pass the day by looking at T.V., and they go out on the porch and talk and different things like that. Especially on holidays the relatives come and carry them home, maybe overnight, two or three days sometimes. Physical therapy isn't available right now. So, like with Jinny (she can't walk by herself), I walk her up and down the hall and around the porch and different places like that.

I hope everybody is going to stay, that this is their home. Everybody seems to be happy. I enjoy myself. I enjoy working with them, and all of them are very nice. There haven't been no problems.

Jinny Young · 73 · Resident of Restful Place · "If I could change things what would I do? I would get up from here and try and do some work around here. You know how a farmer is. A farmer don't sit down . . . but . . . I cain't stand up by myself."

Miss Young never married but lived with her mother who died twenty years ago. She then moved into her brother's home and raised his seven children. Until a recent hospitalization for an operation on a spinal cord tumor, she had been living with her favorite niece, her brother's youngest daughter. She was discharged from the hospital to a nursing home and then to Mrs. Nichols' old age home, Restful Place, where she had been a resident for three months at the time of our visit. A wizened, little black woman she sat in a wheelchair throughout our interview looking rather forlorn. The fingers of both hands were permanently bent due to contracture of the muscles; the doctor told her it was arthritis and rheumatism mixed together.

I reckon I've been here in the rest home going on 'bout three months. I was living with my niece and her husband before I got sick. All the rest of my people beside my brother and myself is dead. My mother has been dead over twenty years and then I stayed with my brother. His wife died when my niece and the other children was small and I had to stay and take care of them. Then my brother drowned when the children were getting into the teen ages. The Lord help me brought them on up and they all got grown and married and got homes of their own. My niece, Ethel Jean, is my brother's seventh daughter.

They put me in the Mill Town hospital first. I don't know what was wrong with me. Practically everything, I reckon. After the hospital I stayed at Flower Nursing Home a long, long time. I got use to everything. I sure did hate to leave. I don't know why I came here. The doctor said I was too well to stay at Flower Nursing Home. And I say I wasn't well enough to go home. So he sent me here.

I wasn't well when I was living with my niece. The doctors had done found something when I went to the hospital, on my spinal cord taking the use away from my legs and arms. And I had to have an operation on my head and neck and shoulders. I still cain't walk by myself; I have to have somebody to walk with me. I don't know if I'll stay here. I tell them sometimes I get homesick, I tell them I'm going home.

But one reason I don't go home is 'cause Ethel Jean, my niece, works over here at Hardees and her husband works all the time. And that's all there is, her husband and her. I goes home on holidays and stay till Sunday, sometimes Monday, and then come back. My niece and her husband usually come every other week about. They are taking care of 'bacco now. So she ain't been now in a pretty good while. But when they get that 'bacco in the house, they will come every other week. I talk to them sometimes on the telephone and I was aiming to call Ethel Jean last week, but my mind told me it wasn't any use to call 'cause she was out on the farm taking care of 'bacco, so I didn't call.

I like it all right since I got here and got use to things around here. I like it all right. Except when I was out in Flower Home we had church, but since I left Flower Home I don't have no church at all. My church is in the country. I want to go so bad sometimes I feel like crying, but I cain't go.

If I could change things what would I do? I would get up from here and try to do some work around here. You know how a farmer is. A farmer don't sit down. I would get up from here and try to work. Make beds and sweep floors and lots of things here need to be done, but I cain't do it. I cain't stand up by myself. I wish I was able to work, and I wish I was able to go home too. I ain't able to work, and the doctor say I ain't able to go home.

Myrtle Evans · Owner of Holly Rest Home · "Mrs. Karakis, she doesn't seem to really think for herself, and it's a shame."

Mrs. Evans operates a Family Care Home and boards four white women in two rooms of the house where she lives with her husband and her daughter of seventeen. We had come to visit Mrs. Karakis, one of the residents, but found it impossible to conduct an uninterrupted, coherent interview with her because Mrs. Evans insisted on answering questions for her, and Mrs. Karakis was obviously unable to comfortably or attentively participate in the conversation. During the time we attempted to speak with Mrs. Karakis, she alternately wept, stuck her fingers in her mouth, or covered her face with her hands. Mrs. Evans kept asking her to uncover her face or to take her fingers out of her mouth. We finally decided to conduct the interview with Mrs. Evans alone.

I've always gotten along well with old people. Even as a little child, I used to go visit the older ladies in the neighborhood—the grandmas. I was unfortunate, I never had a grandmother. She died before I could remember her. So I had a lot of old ladies in the neighborhood I used to go visit. I like babies, too. I had a day-care center for children when my daughter was young. Sometimes, I regret that I quit. But we'd been interested for several years off and on in this type of home for older people. I had several friends who do have this type of home, so we converted our house on Spring Road to accommodate four women. It is confining work of course. That's the biggest problem, and it's even getting worse to get anybody to relieve you, but I'm hoping to find somebody. We own a farmhouse on Creek Road; my husband's been remodeling it, and when he gets through, I hope to find someone to at least sleep in here and let me sleep at home, and just work over here in the daytime. I'd like to find somebody to live in here so that I'd be free to take the ladies to the doctor and, of course, you'd have your hands full just doing that and getting their medication and grocery shopping and running the errands.

My daughter who's almost seventeen, she helps me a little bit. Since school started, though, she had another job, so it's a little bit rough here lately. But as it happened, right after we opened this home, my husband got sick to where he couldn't work his regular job. He still was able to help me here, though, which worked out very nice.

I've had, I'd say, two or three people sent here from nursing homes. Of course, I haven't had much of a turnover here in the two and a half years I've been here. I've had to send two people to a nursing home, because we don't have nursing care or bed patients. Mrs. Karakis has been here about two years, I reckon. She was a bed patient for awhile, but I kept her because it upset her to talk about going back to a nursing home, and the Social Service had agreed they weren't going to put her in a nursing home as long as I was satisfied to keep her. But, you know, it's all according to the person, whether you can keep them or not.

Mrs. Karakis doesn't talk much about herself, but her niece has told me that her first husband was a very, very cruel man. He beat her. She's a person that would let anyone run over her if they would. That's the pathetic thing, and I don't know how long she suffered under that until she left him and went to New York, and there she met Mr. Karakis. He evidently thought a lot of her and took her back to Ashton. They ran a grocery store. Evidently, she was very happy with him. She had a house here, in Mill Town, and she came back and lived in it alone after he died. But due to her health problems her nephew put her in a nursing home, because she would fall out at times, and they'd go in and have to break in the house and find her—she would've had a little stroke.

It's really a shame. They found a buyer for her house, and I feel like probably she got took on that. I don't even know what the house looks like; all I know is they sold her house for three thousand. You see, the nephew and the niece, whatever they'd say, she does. Whatever any of them would say to do, she does. I don't know how they did it, but the nephew and his wife came out here a year ago and told her that it was the doctor's orders, she had to go back to the nursing home. Well, she went out there and she cried that night and she wouldn't eat. She said, "Tell Mrs. Evans to come and get me." Mrs. Karakis, she doesn't seem to really think for herself, and it's a shame.

The one nephew that she raised—she raised that nephew just like her own child and trusted him—he's the one that took advantage of her. He hasn't been to see her, because he knows that she knows that he took her money. He and his wife would tell Mrs. Karakis that she didn't have no more money, but you see they were using it for their own self. Mrs. Karakis and her sisters didn't get along very well. She said there was years when the one who lives near here, if they met on the street one of them would cross the street. But I think now in their old days they love each other and would really like to be together. Her niece, Minnie, visits quite often.

Mrs. Karakis shares a room with Nora. Nora is retarded and she works at the workshop over a year now—it's helped her a lot. They look at television— it's Nora's television—and Nora has it on from the time she comes in from the workshop. Mrs. Karakis seems to be satisfied to look at what Nora wants to every night.

Mrs. Karakis is the most cheerful person in the house, really. She only cries when you get on certain subjects. When anyone comes in to ask her these questions, it makes her think, I guess, of her first husband and these unhappy things.

As we left the Holly Rest Home, Mrs. Karakis, who was sitting on the porch, stopped us and spoke. "They nice to you here and they do things for you, but it is a rest home."

Ellen Whitfield · 82 · "I make a very good old home nurse. I grew up doing that. Rocking the cradle is what I started out with."

Mrs. Whitfield is short with narrow sloping shoulders and thick waist. Her hands are gnarled and her feet and ankles swollen by arthritis, but her face remains delicately attractive. Blue eyes, fair, smooth skin and small fine features are framed by a cap of soft white hair.

Still bright, cheerful and talkative, Mrs. Whitfield lives in a private retirement home, where she has been for the last seven years. While the home is sponsored by an international organization, each local branch chooses its own particular project. In Mill Town 200 women belong to this organization and have chosen to run a retirement home for Christian women as their voluntary effort. The home is fifty years old, situated in an excellent section of Mill Town, meticulously kept and supervised by the local group. There is room for thirty-five women who have single rooms but share bathrooms. Common rooms are well furnished and spacious. Rates are subsidized and range from $385 to $405 a month which includes room, full board and laundry. There is usually a waiting list and applicants are screened by an Admissions Committee. Residents must be well enough to take care of themselves and must be ambulatory. The home has an extremely good reputation in the community.

Mrs. Whitfield enjoys living in Princess Home. Before retiring there she had spent most of her life looking after relatives or friends.

Well, it is an international organization, the Princess Home is. There was two or three wealthy women, I suppose, in New York City that wanted to do some good work for charity and they got this organization started. And of course it was slow at first, but it developed on and we have this home here, and there are others scattered all over the world. There's a book here in our library that will tell you all about it. And of course we have to pay what we think is a big price now for room and board, but everybody says it's as fair a price as we can get anywhere, and we do get good food. We have about three maids in the kitchen all the time. And then we have a night attendant here all night long; she's supposed to be up, dressed, and to go over the building every hour on every floor. We don't keep people who are bedridden for too long. If they get very sick, of course they go to the hospital, and from there to the convalescent homes for a while, and then back here. I like it here. Everything is real nice. We get good food and Mrs. Richardson, the superintendent, if anybody get sick now she's going to call the doctor, and if he says maybe you better get them to the hospital, away we go.

You can bring your own furniture here, but I didn't. I had broken up my home a long time ago—my husband didn't live but twelve years after we were married. When he died I went to live with two brothers in Ashton. We got a house, the three of us, and my youngest sister was with us too. I'm eighty-two years old, and I came here in '69 when I retired. At my age I felt like I didn't want to buy a ramshackle piece of furniture, but I didn't want to put a whole lot of money into furniture either, when I might not live a year.

When my brothers and sister got married and left me alone, I went to look after an aunt for seventeen years and from there to other people, mostly relatives, who needed a companion nurse. I make a very good old home nurse. I grew up doing that. Rocking the cradle is what I started out with. We had a big family. My mother had twelve children, two sets of twins. I was the oldest girl, and I was the one that had that cradle to rock. I was just a little thing. When I was six years old my first little sister came, and I thought that was something dropped down from heaven. I had three brothers and she was the first sister. And so all the way up, my mother was the type that like to get out and kinda do things, and if I just rocked that cradle and stayed with the little ones she was satisfied. So I just fell into that.

When I got into my seventies my brothers didn't want me to go on working and I put my name down on the waiting list for the Princess Homes. I like it here. We are all old and curious and just like children again all over. Still we do just fine I think.

Well, I'll tell you now how I pass the time. I'm not trying to pat myself on the shoulder, but I've been deeply interested in studying the Bible. And I've been doing that more than anything else. And I have an encyclopedia, I have dictionaries, and I have a lot of these books that Billy Graham sends to you. It's all helpful and I have really enjoyed studying the Bible. I've tried to teach Sunday school class one Sunday in the month. We have four teachers, but I keep up with all the lessons. I have a car, but I don't drive wherever I want to because I'm afraid to. There is so much meanness everywhere, that I have gotten so that I just drive when it is necessary. I go to church on Sunday. This church is on the road back out to Ashton. I found out there was plenty of parking space, and there was no steps to climb up.

I have lost my equilibrium—that's my trouble. I don't suffer any pain. I have arthritis and get stiff and all that, but I don't have any pain from it. But I have lost my equilibrium. This morning out there this lady was with me, and I started across the street and I had my cane, but I would reach up and get a hold of her arm. I said, "Rachel, you don't realize how my balance is needed." And she said, "Yes I do too."

Lord, I'm giving you my whole life's history! I don't think there is anything particular that I would crave to be doing, I really don't. I haven't demanded, if I should put it that far, asked, or even wished for too much. If I went to take care of somebody, I wanted to do the best I could. I don't mean to be patting myself on the shoulder, but I've wished a lot of times that everybody wanted to be and tried to be as honest as I do. I've always remembered my father and mother used to tell us all these things. And I remember my aunt, my father's only sister, talking one day and she said, "Well, we all try to do the best we can and then we fail," but she also said, "I do feel like that we all know to be honest."

"Now also when I am old and grayheaded, O God forsake me not."

Psalms 71

afterword

The book is done, the voices now printed words sent to reach unknown readers. I have learned much and been changed by my experience. I was often angry, frustrated by an arrogance, a lack of understanding, a lack of compassion, by the rich for the poor, the powerful for the powerless, the strong for the weak, the young for the old.

At the end I am left not with despair about the uncertain ending of these lives and the almost certain concomitant suffering of their last years. Rather I am overcome by their steadfast courage in adversity, by their independence, their endurance, their faith, their love of nature, family, friends, their will to survive. Old, sick, frail, poor they may be, but the world to them is a beautiful place, and life is worth fighting for to the very end.

We should acknowledge their courage, strengthen their resolve, ease their hardships, fight with them to preserve their independence, enable them to maintain their dignity when facing death. It has been done in other countries; it can be done in ours.

For me the task has just begun. I will use my voice to relay their voices whenever I can. In the Talmud it is written: "It is not for you to finish the task, but neither are you free to abandon it."

4

8

II

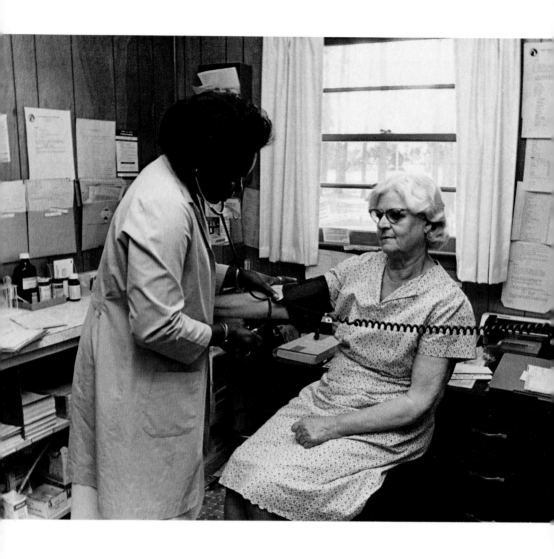

17

24

photographs

Numbers 2, 3, 4, 5, 6, 7, 8, 9, 10, 11, 21, 22, 23, 24, 25, 26, 27, 28 photographed by Dominic D'Eustachio, Ph.D.

Numbers 1, 12, 13, 14, 15, 16, 17, 18, 19, 20, 29, 30 photographed by Duncan Heron, Ph.D.